HOW I LIVED THE
AMERICAN DREAM

DONALD
EUGENE
MOORE

Advantage | Books

Unless otherwise noted, scripture quotations are from the New Scofield Reference Bible, Authorized (King James) Version, copyright © 1967 by Oxford University Press. Used by permission. All rights reserved.

Scripture taken from the New King James Version®. Copyright © 1982 by Thomas Nelson. Used by permission. All rights reserved.

Published by Advantage, Charleston, South Carolina.
Member of Advantage Media.

ADVANTAGE is a registered trademark, and the Advantage colophon is a trademark of Advantage Media Group, Inc.

Printed in the United States of America.

10 9 8 7 6 5 4 3 2 1

ISBN: 978-1-64225-778-6 (Hardcover)
ISBN: 978-1-64225-777-9 (eBook)

LCCN: 2023902598

Book design by Analisa Smith.

THIS BOOK IS DEDICATED TO

Christina, my strong, beautiful, and wonderful wife, who allowed me the time and gave me the space to grow and flourish as I lived out my entrepreneurial dreams. Thank you for always believing in me. I am truly blessed. You have made this an extremely joyful journey! I love you.

Ashley, my beautiful and intelligent daughter, you are wise beyond your years, which makes you the great communicator in my eyes and to the world you live and work in every day. You force me to think, you keep me humble, you keep me honest. You and your family are the source of my joy. My life is truly better because you are in it.

Brandon, my astute, wise, and discerning son, with your wit and charm and commonsense approach, I watch in awe as you live out every day filled with new adventures. You are my real-life architect, with a sense of logic that never ceases to amaze me by what I see you accomplish daily. You are what I aspired to be all those years ago. You are the light of my life.

Madelyn and Sophia, the next generation, I am so lucky and blessed to have you both in my life! You are the future and the present all in one. Although you are too young to know, at this writing I want to thank you for your love and the simple act of being a part of my story of a life.

Steve, my son-in-law, with your academic curiosity and fun-loving personality, you bring a special joy to our world. Thank you for joining the family and for sharing your wonderful daughters, our granddaughters, so freely with us. They are the ray of hope and sunshine in a world that needs more of both.

My family, my life begins and ends with you! Together, you are my reasons for all that I do. It is you who will carry on, proving every day that I existed.

I love you all!

CONTENTS

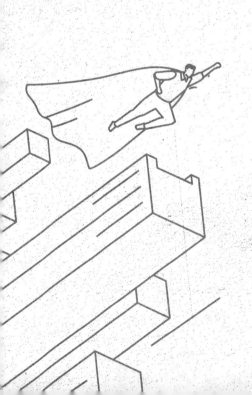

FOREWORD

Anyone who has imagined being the leader of their own fate instead of an unwilling passenger on the corporate merry-go-round will be guided and, more importantly, inspired as Don shares his journey to find his American dream. Don brings his decades of business acumen to the pages of this book, sharing his personal trials and successes and the "Channel Markers" he has developed to help you navigate through your own journey to your American dream, regardless of the business you're in.

I have had the privilege of knowing Don for over thirty years, as a close friend, an employee, a coworker, and an employer. As coworkers, we cut our teeth on the cobblestones of Wall Street in NYC. Then, as the chief operating officer of an internet start-up, the first person I hired was Don. Later, I became the COO at his remarkable creation, VANQUISH.

I have seen Don raise a beautiful family with his lovely wife, Chris, and I have watched him raise an amazing company out of nothing but his own absolute grit. Don's unrelenting determination to achieve his dream is unmatched. I will share this: you better get up early and pack a lunch if you're going to outwork Don Moore.

1

Entrepreneurial journeys are always full of detours and pivots, and events seldom go exactly as planned. Don shares his ups, his downs, and his pivots while illustrating prior lessons he drew from to solve his unexpected detours and manage his company's eventual hypergrowth. I can't think of a better-placed person to help you confront the status quo in pursuit of a greater version of your own life.

Here's to your success!

—STEVE SCHOEPFER

INTRODUCTION

I have an enormous amount of respect for people who consider themselves entrepreneurs. It's no secret that, in most cases, tremendous risks are required. In some cases, that risk is rewarded tremendously and sometimes not so much. When it is rewarded, entrepreneurs and the world at large benefit.

Entrepreneurs hire the most people, drive the economy, create innovation, promote research and development, and shape new products and services. They solve problems by developing new solutions and technologies, utilizing existing resources more effectively, and more times than not they do it on shoestring budgets. It has been said that entrepreneurs change or break the traditional thought process by reducing dependency on obsolete methods and forging new ideas into reality.

I consider entrepreneurs to be the pioneers of today's business world. If you are contemplating launching your entrepreneurial journey, are well on your way, or are anywhere in between, my passion and purpose with this book is to help you succeed. I have sacrificed much in my life to achieve my American dream, and along the way I have learned a few things that have allowed me to help many others live their dreams.

————————

Horse and Buggy Days is a painting by the midcentury artist Paul Detlefsen that currently hangs in my office in North Carolina. It captures a young boy, age nine or ten, watching intently while a farrier is shoeing a horse outside of a shop, with a blacksmith inside forging a horseshoe out of red-hot steel in the fire next to his anvil. The scene takes place somewhere in the early 1900s. The boy is barefoot, standing in the dirt, and shaded by a large tree from the summer sun's raw heat. He is wearing blue denim overalls that come just below the kneecaps. A straw hat sits on his head. To his left is a manual hand-style well water pump.

At a very young age—just like I imagine the little boy in the painting is doing—I dreamed of creating something out of nothing. I saw myself, and still do, as both the boy standing and watching in wonder and the blacksmith who takes a piece of metal and shapes it into a useful purpose. This has always been my desire—to build something out of nothing. Over the last twenty years, I've done exactly that through the building of my own business, and I'm fortunate enough now to be living my dream of working at it every single day.

I don't know where you are in life as you read this book, but I believe you can live out your dream too. One of the biggest obstacles that you will have to overcome is to dare to believe in yourself and your big dreams … and be willing to take that leap!

The problem with most stories about instant legends or overnight-success tales is they are really twenty-year successes. It has been said that it takes ten thousand hours to become proficient at something. Building a business is no different. Anyone who promises instant success, in my book, is selling snake oil. Many traits and talents are crucial to success. This book is not so much a how-to handbook or a road map as it is a guide to use in your journey. I assure you that success is well within your reach! Yes, it comes at a price, and that price is hard work. But it is obtainable.

This book does not contain a silver bullet or flavor-of-the-week strategy for you to follow. Instead, it encompasses a set of rules, strategies, and ways to think about your business decisions. Guideposts, so to speak, for your thought process when faced with the inevitable hardships you are destined to deal with as you venture into the world of entrepreneurship for yourself. I offer you no magic potions. No sleight of hand card tricks to outdo the competition. I do promise you real-life, hands-on experiences that I have lived through, and as a result, I have developed a rule-based guide, a manual of sorts, from my years of practical presuppositions.

What I do is not rocket science; it is actually quite simple, in that twenty years ago, I saw a problem in the electric utility industry, and I set out to offer a solution to that problem. In this book I will share my story about dreaming, having faith, and learning to do whatever it takes to make it work. I will share what I have learned by showing up every day and giving it all I had, even when it looked like it was never going to go my way. You will learn what I thought about as the tables turned for me, against me, and then back in my favor again. I will also talk about how I dealt with the problems, as well as the success, that come with building and owning your own business.

At a young age, I learned to seek out examples of other people who had what I called *great success*. People who were living the dreams I wanted to live. I began to read and study what they did to achieve that success. I wanted to know the cause-and-effect patterns that those people had in common. What actions were behind their achievements so that I could figure how to replicate them, to apply them to my life.

You will understand the thought processes I used in my decision-making, and I will show you how to "be there before you get there." I will define my meaning of the entrepreneur's muscle memory. Most of all, I will give you my insights from the lessons learned in living the American dream, each and every day.

Guy Clark, an American folk and country singer-songwriter, along with Jim Janosky and Susanna Wallis Clark, wrote and released, in 2001, a song via Sony/ATV Music Publishing LLC. That song found its way into my path. It is about a young boy who instinctively believed that life is just a leap of faith: "He did not know he could not fly, and so he did … by trusting his cape!"

I believe life is a leap of faith. I also believe you have to "trust your cape," and that's exactly what I did, even though others told me that building my specific business was impossible. "You cannot do it!" I was told over and over. Yet I did—and I did it in a big way.

CHAPTER ONE

You Can Do Anything, but Not Everything

The two most important days in your life are the
day you are born and the day you find out why.

—MARK TWAIN

In August 2001, about twenty days before two planes would fly into the World Trade Center buildings and forever change the future for millions of Americans, I was in my New York City office at JAGFN, a short-lived streaming financial news network, operating out of a TV studio in the Chelsea district of the city. I looked up as my boss came in and closed the door behind him. I knew this was serious. It has always been an internal problem for me, a deep-seated fear comes over me when someone comes into my office, closes the door behind them, and starts the conversation with the words "We need to talk."

It doesn't matter if they are my superior or my subordinate; either way I instantly panic. Today was no different.

Steve looked me straight in the eyes and said, "JAGFN is done. The business model is not working out as we planned. You know that, and you need to look for something else to do with your career. The future is not here anymore, for either of us."

I knew he was right. JAGFN was a company formed in 2000 with the intent of supplying streaming financial news over computers. We were truly ahead of our time; today there is any number of news, financial information, and programming streamed over the internet daily. But in 2001, we were one of the first in this space. Most of us came from a financial background. And so we were positioned to know what Wall Street would want from a streaming financial news program. Our sister company, Jagnotes, had been supplying early-morning financial news on individual companies traded on the stock exchanges for years with great success. As the television commercial goes, we knew a thing or two about financial markets, and their insatiable need for ahead-of-the-market news streaming right to your desktop or laptop computer, as it happens, was a no-brainer for us.

I had left my position as a financial advisor at the Smith Barney office located in Lawrenceville, New Jersey, to move my career to JAGFN. It was a move up for me. Stock options, a good paycheck, a chance to work in the Big Apple and to be on the cutting edge of the newest technology available on what was relatively a new concept at the time, the World Wide Web, or as we call it today, the internet.

I was officially the head of business development. But my responsibilities encompassed a whole host of tasks beyond building new business relationships for our company. I have never been one to step away from a challenge, and so I also carried the responsibilities associated with technology, customer subscriptions, show distribution, and website management to include the relationships we had with the hosting, streaming, and design companies who performed the backend functionality of the websites and the video players people accessed to view our programming.

Our downfall as a company, and the reason Steve was in my office, was not because he and I were failing in our responsibilities. The problems were bigger than both of us. The infrastructure and distribution chains for streaming media and the bandwidth costs were relatively new platforms and came with obstacles that we just ran out of money and time on. On our start-up budget, we could not overcome the relative ease TV had with these details. We simply could not stream in an acceptable quality on the bandwidth size available in comparison to television and the likes of CNBC. We worked with the giants at the time, Yahoo Finance and Lycos News. We hired well-known anchormen and a top-notch producer. Unfortunately, the stock market players shorted our stock and left us between a rock and a hard place when it came to raising funds for the shows we produced. We had great guests and good commentary, but we just ran out of time when the dot-com bubble burst. Steve, myself, the team, and JAGFN became collateral damage.

I had heard similar words from bosses like Steve before in my various career paths. The truth be told I had known it for

> **I had tied my family's future to this job, to this new career path.**

almost a year now, and yet I tried my best to deny it. I took this job because I believed this was the big one, the ticket to prosperity and success. The fulfillment of all my hopes, dreams, and aspirations. Once again, I had tied my family's future to this job, to this new career path.

Steve told me to pack up my things and take them home with me that weekend. I could work from home for now, but I should dust off my résumé and start a vigorous search for a new place for my career to call home. The company was on life support, and there was no telling how long the powers that be could keep it going.

That night, as I sat for dinner with my family, I knew I was facing the proverbial two paths that diverged in the woods, unsure of where either would take me. In the past, whenever I'd heard Steve's words, "The future is not here anymore," like most people, I would panic. But I now needed to ask myself, "Do I stay on the road most traveled and become an employee at yet another company, or do I take the one less traveled and invest in myself to truly find out where my magic is?"

At age fifty-two, Ray Kroc, the founder of McDonald's, and my hero, was still looking for the magic—something that would allow him to capitalize on his three decades of sales experience. John Love writes in his book *McDonald's: Behind the Arches* that Ray was convinced he had finally found his once-in-a-lifetime opportunity. "It was practically life or death for me," Kroc said. "If I lost out on McDonald's, I'd have no place to go."

The magic.

Ray Kroc found it in McDonald's. But for me, like a needle in a haystack, it was something I had been searching for throughout my career that seemed impossible to find. Yet I knew that once I found the magic, I would have the source of my passion. I looked for it every time I changed jobs or career paths. I would pour my life into this new avenue, hoping, praying that this was to be the one that made me come alive, where what I was doing was effortless because it was rooted within me.

By 2001, at age forty-two, I was still looking for my magic—something I was created for, something I could build, something I could call my own. An enterprise that would allow me to fulfill my hopes and dreams and provide for my family the way I always believed I should.

I had heard people say "I came into this world at the right time, and I am going to go out at the right time." If they were right, then the gap between the two "right times" was my life, and I didn't want to waste the time that had been given to me. I needed to sort through the distractions and dig deep into myself. The sad truth for most adults is that life's responsibilities have a way of killing the magic. But I wanted to do what felt right to me and to find my mission in life. I knew I had something to accomplish because I believed that's how my Creator had made me.

———————

"Why does this happen to me?" How many times have you heard that question from others? How many times have you asked that question yourself?

I have come to believe people are defeated in life not because of a lack of their ability but, more often than not, for their lack of wholeheartedness. A lack of wholeheartedness includes feeling sorry for yourself, feeling you got the short end of the stick in life, feeling that life has conspired against you, and worst of all, feeling that you don't deserve to succeed.

When my daughter, Ashley, and my son, Brandon, were younger, I had many things I felt were my duty to teach them. Lessons to live by. The keys to life that I would share with them, on way too many occasions, I am sure. But the point was to guide them in their decision-making processes with simple and easy-to-understand check points.

For example, "First things first." I had said that so many times my son would repeat it to me every time we started a project. I would look at him as we stood before the subject of our focus, and he would look up at me and say "Got it, Dad. First things first!" You see, I had taught him that we needed to make a list of what was required to success-fully complete the undertaking at hand. The point I was making: it is important to size up the task, determine what you need to accomplish the mission, then go about getting everything before you start. Those who start and make several trips to the toolbox, the hardware store, or wherever, waste valuable time. If you are going to do the job right, it is important to think about it *first* and get an answer or a plan for everything you can think of that you will find necessary to succeed. Another was "Don't build a box of responsibility until you are ready to live in it." I explained to my children that when we start out, our lives are limitless—we are not trapped. We can do anything and go anywhere. I would explain that the world had a whole host of pos-sibilities for them to explore. Endless opportunities. They could do anything their hearts desired in life. I went on to explain that when you buy a car with a car payment, you put up a wall. When you decide to get married, you put up another wall. When you buy a house, you add an additional wall. All these become walls of responsibility. When you add children to the mix, you add another wall, and in very short order, you find yourself in life's box that you intentionally or unintentionally built for yourself.

Not that any of those things are bad things in and of themselves, but together you have put yourself into a position of having to deal with today's responsibilities and therefore limiting your ability to do other things. The lesson I wanted them to take away was that you can do anything but you cannot do everything. So choose wisely.

That is precisely where I stood at age forty-two. I could do almost anything, as my résumé showed. But I had to decide what I was going to do right then and there—that day.

It has been my experience that most people have a variety of excuses when it comes to why they will not or cannot do something. If times were different, or perhaps if they were born into a different place, a different family, or earlier in history—there never seems to be an end to the litany of reasons why we put our dreams on hold.

"I don't have enough money." "When I make more money or have more money, I will give it a try." "I have a family to support. There is no time for me to start my own business." "There is more to life than hard work, and I need balance." "My family needs me home right now." "When the kids are older, I will devote time to my dreams." All of these are excuses—perfectly well-accepted excuses that no reasonable person would argue with. Yes, you are correct, this is not the right time to live your life, your dreams, because you are too busy living your life with today's reality—until the day comes when you are told the end of this career path has just happened.

I believe that life gives us every opportunity to put our dreams in a box and stuff them up in the attic or hide them in the basement. The conversation with Steve was such a time—a time to box up what you are, reduce the accomplishments in your life to two pages, and start the search for what to do next. A time to once again reinvent yourself to prove to someone somewhere that you are valuable and that you have something to offer.

I knew I had a lot to offer another organization, but truth be told I was burned out on the thought of having to start over again somewhere new. New people, new dreams, new goals, new ideas … all someone else's. Not mine.

I am one of those people who accept a challenge very easily. I can be set on fire and burn for almost any new opportunity. I am the first in and the last out of most everything I do. But it was getting tiresome, this reinvention process for what seemed like my entire life. I cringed at the thought of once again having to do it. I had done it so many times in the last twenty-two years. I dreaded doing it again.

———————

Ruminating on the instructions from my boss on that fateful day in August—when he told me to dust off my résumé and start a vigorous search for a new place for my career to call home—I started reliving the same emotions I had waded through back in October of 1976, my senior year in high school. It was the time of year when students met with their guidance counselor to discuss their future. Would you go to college? If so, where would you apply? What would you study? All decisions to be discussed in detail, culminating with the drawing up of a plan laying out the way forward. You were to come out of that meeting with your marching orders.

I fancied myself a student of architecture in those days. I had the good fortune of attending a very good public high school with an exceptional architectural program. I had taken all the available elective courses and maintained an A average in each drawing class. I loved drawing and designing. I wanted to build something someday, and it was going to be magnificent. There was no doubt.

I was heart-struck for a girl back in high school who was in my drawing classes. I remember helping her with her drawing assignments from time to time. I would even complete some of her turn-in work now and then. On one such occasion, we had the same assignment, and even though my submission was a slightly different solution than hers, she received an A for her efforts, and I received a B. When I inquired of the teacher why this could possibly happen—careful not to let the fact slip that I had done both assignments—he simply explained that, for her, the work she submitted was an A-quality presentation. The work on my submission was a B-quality drawing for my talents. In the years since then, I've always said that, as a kid, whoever told you that life should be fair was lying! Lesson learned.

To compound the matter, just a few days before my meeting with the guidance counselor, I attended a career day for architecture students held at Princeton Day School. It was hosted by a locally famous architect in the Princeton area. He would invite all the architecture students in the county to attend. All attendees were presented with a problem in advance: to design a basic layout and a three-point perspective drawing set for a bank on a downtown location—without cutting down a single tree on the property. Upon arrival, we were required to submit our solution, which then would be critiqued by the staff of his firm. This meant we were given a week to prepare a drawing set for submission.

On the morning of the event, my girlfriend informed me that she had not done the assignment. After lecturing her on how she could not possibly attend such an event and not have a submission, I drew her submission for her on a drawing board, propped up by the steering wheel, in the front seat of my dad's pickup truck, in thirty minutes, while she watched. We parked out back of the municipal building so no one would see what I was doing.

Upon arrival at the Princeton Day School, we turned in our drawings and proceeded to jump from lecture to lecture for the balance of the morning. This gave the staff ample time to review our drawings and solutions. After lunch, we assembled in the auditorium. I don't remember how many hundreds of students were in attendance, but taped to the white board at the head of the room were six drawings. Two of which were hers and mine. As the architect in charge critiqued the solutions, we all got exceptionally high marks and, more importantly, high recognition. Obviously, what excited me was technically getting praise on both of the submitted solutions—one painstakingly prepared and the other done in a rush that morning in the front seat of a pickup truck. Further cementing in my mind that I had what it took to be an architect. As a result, the six of us were invited to interview at the host architect's firm for a summer internship. Just in case you were wondering, no, she did not get the internship. But neither did I.

At school the following week, Mr. Morris was my guidance counselor for the task of the "What are you going to do with your life?" talk. I knew of him, but I had never actually dealt with him before. He had a reputation of being a straight shooter, a man's man, a no-bullshit kind of guy. Somehow the luck of the draw put me in front of him. So here I was, walking into his office, and he motioned for me to sit in the wooden chair stationed in front of his desk, located inside the small concrete block office he inhabited in the guidance department of Hopewell Valley Central High School in Pennington, New Jersey.

He had my folder in front of him, closed on the desk. When I was seated, he said, "So tell me, what do you want to do with your life?"

I was ready for him. I stated very clearly and very self-confidently, "I am going to be an architect. I want to go to Clemson University in South Carolina, my first choice. Or Syracuse University in New York, my second choice. And my safety school, just in case, is Texas A&M. All three schools have great architecture programs." I didn't say it, but I remember thinking that any school would be lucky to have me because I was the next world-famous Frank Lloyd Wright.

Mr. Morris, if he was impressed with my self-confidence, didn't show it. He just leaned forward and opened the folder on his desk. He thumbed through the content as he studied the pages one by one, with no expression. After what seemed like a very long time, he closed the folder. Slowly he moved it to the top of a pile of other student folders to his left. He leaned back in his chair, looked me right in the eyes, and said, "I think we need to look for a good trade school for you."

I could feel my heart explode in my chest. I was angry! I stared at him red faced, then shouted, "What? I'm a damn good architecture student!"

With the weight of those few words uttered by my guidance counselor, Mr. Morris, my dream of becoming a famous architect began its descent into the death spiral of life.

Responding to my outburst, Mr. Morris crossed his arms and said, "You do know your grades, right?"

He went on to explain that even though I had an A in gym and an A in architecture, that was not enough. My transcripts would not even be considered by the colleges of my choice. Even the local community college would require I take remedial courses before they would consider me. His last words to me that day were "I know a welder in town; maybe he will teach you to weld. You can make a good living as a welder." Feeling defeated, I respectfully thanked him, then walked out of his office.

That night after dinner, when the table was cleared, I turned to my dad and said, "I have been thinking, maybe I should postpone college for a year and come to work for you." I remember my dad looking at me for only what seemed like a brief second. Then, yelling out to my mother—who had relocated to the kitchen with the dirty dishes—he said, "Alberta, I told you the kid wasn't going to college." He got up from the table and walked away, and that is where the conversation ended. The possibility of me becoming an architect was never to be spoken about again.

As I think back to that time, I realized that as painful as that day was for me to come to terms with the fact that I would never become an architect, I was going to be more than okay. But in that moment, I was learning some of the most valuable lessons: Life is what we make it. Life is a result of what we do

> ## As painful as that day was ... I was going to be more than okay.

or don't do; how much we put in versus how much we take out; that 20 percent of effort is never enough. One hundred percent is needed, and in some cases, even more than that will not be enough. There are times when we need to put in more than we take out if we want to reap the benefits down the road.

More importantly, I have come to find out that when one door closes, another truly does open ... we just need to be looking for it with patience.

I have always considered myself to be self-aware. I evaluate my actions and my thoughts regularly. Even as a young person, I would contemplate the future and the opportunities that God, the universe, and the world offered me. I realized that day that being an architect was not going to be one of them. You could argue that the circumstances of my life up until that meeting in the guidance office were the reasons. I knew the truth. I was defeated that day not because of my lack of ability but for my lack of wholeheartedness. And whole-

22

heartedness was something that I had to learn, if I was to find, and fulfill, my passion in life.

In my current situation, I was about to, once again, be unemployed and searching for my magic, and so none of that history seemed to matter. I was emotionally drained and bone tired of starting over on some new career path at some new job in some new profession.

I remember talking to my wife, Christina, that mid-August night, after Steve had uttered his infamous words to me earlier in the day. We had been married for sixteen years at that time—I explained to her that this might be my last chance to make something happen, while trying to encourage myself not to give up. I desperately needed to find the magic. I needed to convince her—to convince myself—that it was time for us, for me, to take the chance and invest in myself. Deep in my heart, I knew this was true, but mentally, I was burned out, and the thought of once again molding myself into some new role or taking another new career path seemed overwhelming.

I was done telling myself "This is it. This is the one." Believing in it so hard. Pouring every ounce of myself into it. I couldn't bear the thought of the same thing happening again. That no matter how well I performed, no matter how many promotions and accolades I received, when yet another job ended, I would once again be left empty handed, broken, reliving the memories of what could have been … if only I had done this or said that.

How could I get off the could-have-been train that continually ran through my brain? I had always thought that every job I ever had was going to be my forever job. I believed it every time, that I would happily retire with a thirty-plus-year career. Yet every job ended for one reason or another in what seemed like a statistical cause and effect: Every 3.2 years, Don would be starting over. Mark your calendar.

After hearing my "emotional plea for sanity," Christina very simply, without judgment, asked me, "What will you do?"

I didn't know. I had not thought that far. I was still in the place of convincing myself that it was a good idea to invest in me. It wasn't like we had a lot of money; in fact, we had none. Christina's acceptance of what I was saying had come easy to her. No protest. No fight. She would tell me years later, when I asked why she was so understanding, that it was simply because she always believed in me and my dreams. And that whatever I did, she knew I would be successful. Of that, she had no doubt.

If I was going to answer Christina's question, I needed to identify a business model I could develop. I am a man of simple math. If two and two does not add up to four, I am out. This ability to reduce the situation to its simplest common denominator has served me well over the years. As a result of my years working for many well managed companies, and some mismanaged—as well as the occasional successful and some not-so-successful entrepreneurs—I have made a series of observations on what works and what does not work.

Every job I ever held, regardless of the position, I worked as if I owned the place. I didn't have a prideful attitude but one that told me I needed to do the best job possible. I've been this way since I was a kid, and I did not know any other way to be. I was always fully invested in the company, in the position, and most of all, in me. I believe all of life, the ups and the downs, is a moment to learn. God's gift to our individual education. There is formal education—book smarts; and then there is experience—street smarts, as they say. I believe you need both to succeed. I believe that doing the day-to-day with our best effort is investing in ourselves for the future. It has been said that we are what we think about, and so, for me, I always thought I owned the place so that someday I just might.

From time to time, some forty years later, I am alone with a good cigar, a glass of Jack Daniel's Single Barrel Tennessee Whiskey poured over ice, perched in a chair at the top of a beach cliff on the island of Bermuda, looking out over the continuous roll of the ocean, and I think back on that day of Mr. Morris's chastisement and my dad's dismissiveness and humbly marvel at all I have accomplished. How far I have come in life!

A Bible verse I learned while attending the Calvary Baptist Church in Hopewell, New Jersey, all those years ago aptly fits this time in my life: "but this one thing I do, forgetting those things which are behind, and reaching forth unto those things which are before" (Philippians 3:13b).

Reflecting on Mark Twain's words that open this chapter: even though that day with Mr. Morris, when I sat in his office—and at night with my father at the dining room table—wasn't either of those days for me, those events were both very important mile markers on my road to finding the answer as to why I was born and what I was meant to do.

On that mid-August night, after hearing Steve's words, I stood facing the proverbial two paths that diverged in the woods, still looking for my magic. With my wife Christina's full support, I decided to take the road less traveled. And I can tell you now, that truly has made all the difference for me.

CHAPTER ONE
CHANNEL MARKERS

Author's Note:

The lyrics to Garth Brooks's and Victoria Shaw's song "The River" describes a dream like a river, ever changing as it flows. Never knowing what's in store makes each day a constant battle just to stay between the shores. To that end, I pray that the ideas and thoughts I present within these pages might serve as "channel markers." Channel markers along that river, in hopes of keeping you between the shores as you live out your dream.

First things first.

I have observed so many people spending so much time working inefficiently. My conclusions told me that if I would just take the time to plan, I would accomplish so much more with the relatively short amount of time I have available. When I was in the army, there was a saying: "There is never enough time to do it right, but there is always enough time to do it again."

Don't build a box of responsibility until you are ready to live in it.

I learned this rule the hard way. It is so easy to say yes and so much harder to say no. Bottom line: The more responsibility I accept today directly limits my freedom in the future. Some call this the *opportunity cost*. Or worse, the results of the expectation of immediate gratification.

Go after what I want in life; if I don't, I will never have it.

When I left the army in 1981, I was faced with the question I had heard before and would hear again: "What will you do?" I had to develop the mindset that if I don't pursue what I want, I am sure not to have it. I have got to give it all that I have, and in some cases, more than I have will not be enough. But if I don't try, I will surely never have it.

I will forever remain in the same spot if I don't step forward.

I have met so many people in my life who were afraid to take a chance, to get out of their comfort zone. The only way I was going to get out of the job I did not like or the relationship that was not working was if I made the change, and that change came in the action of moving forward.

Strive to control my future, or someone else will.

My father and the army drove this lesson into my brain. During my early life as a son, as an enlisted man, as an employee, I was living someone else's dream, and I was controlled by them as long as I was beholden to them for my survival.

I must control my own destiny, or someone else will.

I decided it was important for me to find a way to control my own destiny. I did this as best as I could while working for others, but I never truly experienced it until I started my own business. This rule was also inspired by Jack Welch and his mother, who taught it to him.

(Not to be confused with the channel marker above: Controlling my destiny is much bigger than controlling my future!)

I can do anything, but I cannot do everything. I need to choose wisely.

I love the feeling of being able to do anything I want. The reality is that once I start down that path, my options almost always become limited. Therefore, I need to be sure before I start that I really want what I am about to do.

CHAPTER TWO

The Power of Thinking Positively

Have faith in your abilities! Without a humble but reasonable confidence in your own powers you cannot be successful or happy. But with sound self-confidence, you can succeed.

—*NORMAN VINCENT PEALE,* THE POWER OF POSITIVE THINKING *(1952)*

My life began in the small little town of Helmetta, New Jersey, in February of 1959. Twenty days after what would become known as "the day the music died." The final year of the 1950s would see the month of February marked by the tragic deaths of Buddy Holly, Ritchie Valens, and the Big Bopper, along with Roger Peterson, the pilot, when their small plane crashed near Clear Lake, Iowa.

I was born on the morning of the twenty-third day of the month at about twenty minutes past eleven and promptly named Donald

Eugene Moore. *Donald* after my father, and *Eugene* after my mom's father, know to me as Poppy. I was the first child of Alberta Margaret, daughter of Mildred and Samuel Eugene Bonura, wife of Donald George Moore, the son of Emma and George "Chubby" Moore.

My birth occurred at the Middlesex County General Hospital, located in New Brunswick, New Jersey. The hospital still stands today, and through a series of mergers, it is now known as Robert Wood Johnson University Hospital.

Helmetta is where both sets of my grandparents lived. In fact, just a couple of blocks from each other on Old Forge Road. It was where my mother and father grew up, went to school, learned to drive, fell in love, and started what would eventually become a family of seven.

Upon learning of my pending arrival, Dad joined the US Army Quartermaster Corps, headquartered in Fort Lee, Virginia; married Mom; and was almost immediately shipped to South Korea. My mom and I stayed with her parents up to and through the first year of my life. How great it must have been for me: Granny and Poppy lived with my mom and me, and Grandpop and Grandma Moore lived within a quarter mile of us, walking distance, on the same street in small-town, flag-waving America. I am only sorry I was too young to remember it; this is the stuff that dreams and great stories are made from.

When my father returned to Helmetta upon the completion of his military duty assignment in South Korea some thirteen months later, it was to move us across the country to Bisbee, Arizona. He had his orders from Uncle Sam, and Helmetta was not his place of assignment. They told me stories that I did not know him and was quite upset at leaving my grandfather, Poppy, whom I have no doubt I had bonded with that first year. They say I screamed and cried for the whole drive to Arizona. Not a good confidence builder for a nineteen-year-old man who had just met his son for the first time.

Fort Huachuca was his new duty assignment. Located about forty-six miles southwest of the famous town of Tombstone. A town where on October 26, 1881, the Earp brothers faced off against the Clanton-McLaury gang in the legendary shootout at the O.K. Corral. There is an old black-and-white photo floating around my parents' attic. It is of me, just barely old enough to stand, positioned in front of a gravestone located in row six of the famous Boothill Cemetery in Tombstone.

The stone reads

HERE
LIES
Lester Moore
FOUR SLUGS
FROM A 44
NO LES
NO MORE

The story goes that Lester Moore worked at a Wells Fargo office in Naco, Arizona, along the Mexican border. A man named Hank Dunston arrived one day to claim his package. The package was damaged, and Dunston was not happy, so he let the lead from his .44-caliber pistol fly at Lester. Les took four shots to the chest but managed to get his own shot off at Dunston as he fell. The Wells Fargo clerk ended up with the most famous epitaph on Boothill. Nobody knows where the disgruntled customer is buried.

Together, my dad and the army dragged our growing family, with the addition of my sister Susan and little brother Thomas, across the country, as he was assigned to various posts in Korea; France; Virginia; Arizona; and finally, Fort Benning, Georgia, where he and the US Army parted company. Back to the small little town of Helmetta we went, where my brother Edward arrived just before Christmas in 1964.

My parents rented the caretaker's house located on the estate at 11 High Street in Helmetta. The estate was originally owned by George W. Helme, a former New Orleans lawyer and major general in the Confederate army. The story goes that in 1880, George bought land between Jamesburg and Spotswood along the Pennsylvania Railroad's Jamesburg branch line, on which to build his snuff mill. Helme is said to have named the town Helmetta after his family surname ("Helme") and his daughter Antoinette ("Etta").

The story goes on to say that while George was sitting on the front porch of his mansion, an employee of the mill stopped by to talk and watched George slump back in the rocker and die of an apparent heart attack. Years later—after reading about Helme and his quest to build the town from two houses along a railroad line and a small mill into five hundred people—the seed was planted in me. He lit the spark that a dreamer like me might build something, someday, that affected other people in a positive way. I didn't dare to think that I would build a town or a mill, but I was sure I would build something worth remembering.

In the summer of 1970, I was eleven years old when my parents loaded our suitcases, sleeping bags, and camping gear, all crammed together on the roof rack of our 1966 Plymouth station wagon. My dad tied it all down as best as could be with bungee cords, rope, and blue tarps. Although we could not see it from inside the car, I am sure our stuff bounced and flapped around on top of the vehicle, all the way to New York State. We were set for a family vacation of camping in the fields of Binghamton and the apple orchards of Rochester.

My parents had planned a week's worth of adventure for us. We would start out working our way northwest to visit high school friends of theirs who were trying their hand at farming, and in so doing had rented a farm in upstate near Binghamton, New York. We would end the week at a campground on the shores of Lake Ontario, in an apple orchard. It was, and still is, one of the greatest family trips we ever took together.

When we arrived at the farm in Binghamton—this sounds foolish even to me as I write this, but it was my belief at the time—I was bored. With the mothers being occupied catching up on things since high school and their attention needed to keep the younger kids engaged, I somehow managed to find myself in the attic of their rented house. I don't think I would have broken in. Let's just say that maybe it was raining outside, and so I must have felt I had free rein over the domain to enter the attic of the old farmhouse on my own.

To my recollection there was not a lot in the attic, certainly not anything compared to movies of people getting lost in the attic for days, exploring. I was there all of about fifteen minutes. The one thing I found was a book,

I cannot swear to you that I read the whole book ... but I did read enough of it to be hooked for life.

which I carried with me as I returned down the attic stairs. The importance of telling you about this book is that I became hypnotized by it. I cannot swear to you that I read the whole book cover to cover on that vacation, but I did read enough of it to be hooked for life.

The book, *The Power of Positive Thinking* by Norman Vincent Peale, was written in 1952, seven years before I was born. As I sat on the plywood floor, I became more and more engrossed in the concepts within its covers: *Believe in Yourself*, *Try Prayer Power*, *Expect the Best and Get It*, and *I Don't Believe in Defeat*.

I was hooked!

My young brain was inspired by Mr. Peale's concepts:[1]

Feelings of confidence depend upon the type of thoughts that habitually occupy your mind. Think defeat and you are bound to feel defeated. But practice thinking confident thoughts, make it a dominating habit, and you will develop such a strong sense of capacity that regardless of what difficulties arise you will be able to overcome them. Feelings of confidence actually induce increased strength.

I remember the feelings inside of me. It was as if I had just discovered the secrets to life—even if I wasn't old enough to realize whether people would even be looking for the secrets to life. I can tell you now with great confidence, finding that book that summer set a foundation of optimism and stick-to-it-ism in me that no matter how dark my life might get, I was sure I would overcome. Even if, at that moment, I had no concept of how dark life can be at times, I was sure, from reading those words on those pages, I was and would continue to be a success, even if I or the world didn't know it yet.

About halfway through the book, Dr. Peale wrote about an instructor coaching a trapeze artist who had suddenly filled with fear of performing on the high-trapeze bar. "I can't do it! I can't do it!" the artist said.

---

1   Norman Vincent Peale, *The Power of Positive Thinking* (New York: Simon and Schuster, 2015), 15.

The coach leaned in and replied, "Throw your heart over the bar and your body will follow."

That simple little statement became seared in my brain: Throw your heart over the bar and your body will follow.

The book set me on a path of positive thinking for the rest of my life. While I know there are pessimistic people in the world who have success, I'm just not one of them. For instance, one of my life mottos is "Expect the best and get it!" It doesn't matter what age you are; I believe you can develop the power of positive thinking in your daily and business life—it comes down to a choice you make. I also believe that you must practice positive thinking daily. Life can be hard, and if you don't start out positive each morning … well, the alternative is to start out negative, and then you will surely be negative all the time.

In the spring of 1971, I was twelve years old, and my parents decided that I should participate in little league baseball. My memory is very clear on this—I was not very good at it. As a result, I did not play much, because I did not hit much and I could not catch much. Not good traits if you want to get playing time. I remember one specific time very clearly. It was on the baseball diamond behind the Bowne School in Old Bridge, New Jersey. I was at bat, and I would like to tell you the count was full, the bases were loaded, and I was about to knock in the winning run—but that is not what happen. What did happen was I said to myself, "This time, you will hit the ball!"

I threw my heart over the bar, and damn, when I swung at the next pitch, I hit the ball! My body shook all the way to my toes and back to my outstretched arms. The sound of the smack of the bat against the ball echoed in my ears. The problem was I had closed my eyes when I swung the bat, and now I stood there in the batter's box.

Time was standing still in my mind. As I realized what I had done, pride swelled in my chest. I did it. I hit the ball. Then, with just short of enough clarity, I heard everyone screaming, "Run, Donald! Run!" Too late. By the time I started to run, the throw went to first, and I was out before I got halfway there.

But I didn't care. I had practiced the power of positive thinking and it had worked. There was no taking that away from me now.

Just in case you are wondering, I did not steal the book. I asked Aunt Julie if I could borrow it, and she said I could have it. Although she gave me a funny look when she read the title.

On the first day of June 1972, my parents moved our family to the small little town of Hopewell, New Jersey. I had three weeks until my sixth-grade classes would end. Just enough time to have me and my siblings enrolled in the new school and to meet a few kids that, in my case, I would spend the next six years with, but not enough time to bond with any of them. I don't honestly think my parents picked the date to move. I truly believe the powers that be set the closing date, and my parents did as they were instructed.

Hopewell is a quaint little town located in a valley in the west central part of New Jersey. It is a small town with a lot of history. Perhaps one of its most famous residents was Mr. John Hart. Who, exactly two hundred years before I sat with Mr. Morris, my guidance counselor, to have the talk about my future, was one of the original signers of the Declaration of Independence. In the 1770s, he had acquired some six hundred acres, making him the largest landowner in Hopewell at the time. His original farmhouse was now, because of the growth of the town over the two-hundred-year time span, located in the borough limits, a few blocks from my parents' new home. As a paperboy I would deliver the local newspaper to the current residents of the house and wonder if they knew the historical value of living in the house built by a signer of the Declaration of Independence all those years ago.

Established in 1756, Hopewell Academy was the first educational institution sponsored by the Baptists in the American colonies. The school educated such men as James Manning, who went on to be the first college president of what is now known as Brown University in Providence, Rhode Island. I cut the grass every week at the widow Holcomb's property on Broad Street, formally the Hopewell Academy, where James Manning studied.

I attended Calvary Baptist Church in town. The lineage of that church went back over two hundred years. In fact, one of the earliest ministers, John Gano, was said to have baptized General George Washington at Valley Forge, when he was one of his chaplains. My affiliation with John Gano's church was deep, as I was baptized there, one of my first jobs was as a sexton for the church, I was the youth representative on the pulpit committee for a time, and I was president of the youth fellowship when I was in high school.

In 1932, Charles Lindbergh and his wife, Anne Morrow Lindbergh, lived on Featherbed Lane, located at the top of a hill overlooking the town of Hopewell, when their twenty-month-old son, Charles Junior, was kidnapped from the nursery of their estate. The story goes that a truck driver discovered the body of the baby when he was stopped to relieve himself in the woods on the opposite hill of the Hopewell Valley. He is said to have told his partner, "It's Tuesday, so the sheriff is in the chair at Ray Cox's barbershop. Let's go tell him what we found."

I sat in that same barber chair as the sheriff while Mr. Raymond Cox cut my hair, every other week for six years. That barber shop and that chair are where I learned about cigars, cigar cutters, types of tobacco, and life from the men who gathered in the barber shop and told their stories. They told tales about the town's history and the people who made something of themselves. All the while, I was breathing in and learning to love the smell of cigars, fostering the desire for and planning to someday smoke cigars while designing great buildings.

I dreamed of someday leaving and then returning to Hopewell. To make my mark as an architect. To build something great.

I graduated from high school in 1977, and I immediately went to work for my father's business as a trailer mechanic. My dad had given up the truck driver life when I was in tenth grade and formed a small business repairing the trailer end of tractor trailers. He and my uncle Jack rented a small Quonset hut just outside of town and proceeded to build a name for themselves. Working for my dad did not last long; by February of 1978, I had enlisted in the army's Military Police Corp and was promptly assigned to an overseas US contingent of NATO troops in Germany. After a three-year stint, I was honorably discharged from the Ninety-Fifth MP Battalion and sent back to the US in February of 1981. Just in time for my twenty-second birthday. By the time I turned forty-two, when I heard Steve's words about my future at JAGFN, my employment record showed a myriad of jobs.

Although I was extremely successful in all my career endeavors, I did have my fair share of them. I had been a truck driver, a trailer repair mechanic, a salesman, a fast-food restaurant employee, a book-keeper, a general manager for a bread crumb manufacturer, a business-development manager, a plant manager for an animal feed plant, an entrepreneur who built race car trailers, a stockbroker at Prudential

Securities, a financial advisor at Smith Barney, and a business-development manager for the financial news network known as JAGFN. Along the way I attended nine years of night school and managed to graduate from a two-year community college earning an associate's degree in accounting. I had earned a bachelor of science degree from Rider University in Lawrenceville, New Jersey. Each of these career paths would come to an end for one reason or another. I would get promoted or raised to the upper end of the position or reach the highest responsibility allowed in the company, and inevitably I would find myself with no advancement opportunities, no growth potential, no magic, and I would need to move on in search of a more challenging role somewhere else.

The good news: twenty-plus years of multiple business exposures and experiences, as well as formal education in accounting and business, would serve me well in the future. Little did I know that I had been "planting seeds" in my life. The bad news: I still hadn't found my magic.

In 1999, while working as a financial advisor at Smith Barney, I belonged to the Rotary Club, in Princeton, New Jersey. We would meet every Tuesday for lunch. Oh, how I enjoyed those times! Part of the admittance process required that I give a speech to the group, introducing myself and sharing my background. My original motive for joining the club was to network with the folks, to prospect without prospecting directly. That would be frowned upon, although everyone, I was sure, did it. I was looking to find new clients, or referrals for new clients, to enrich my financial advisor career. Instead, I learned a greater lesson.

The appointed day came, and it was my turn. I still remember my speech. I tried to keep it light and entertaining. They loved me, and in fact, most of them thought I was making up my life's story. They could not conceive of the fact I had such a variety of jobs. The revelation for me, while listing my past business experiences and past employment experiences, the culmination of which had led me to this place in time, was realizing then and there how many things I had done in my short thirtysomething life. Most of which the audience seated before me could not identify with. That was okay. I was a regular guy who had pursued regular jobs, and they liked me as a well-rounded person who did not come from Princeton ideals and old money. I was a guy from the next town over who grew up and worked hard at a lot of things and wound up in the Princeton circles of life. Which, to be honest, gave them, I believe, a sense of admiration toward me.

Lesson learned while giving my introduction-to-Donald speech, it became clear to me that I must "edit my past" in the future and use the highlights that best accentuate the positives of my experiences, not necessarily the quantity of my experiences. Although I thoroughly entertained them, in that moment I realized that no one would give me an order to buy stocks or to prepare a financial plan for them, because the picture I painted, although successful at my choices, showed that I might not be in that job for very long. My employment history gave the wrong perception of my story, and once I'd told it, I learned immediately that I should not try to sell my services to them because I had inadvertently given them a wrong impression of who I was. So I didn't push for their business. Instead, I pushed myself to be comfortable in an environment that was completely out of my comfort zone. I could be compared to the guy who didn't know which fork to eat his salad with, like the guy who wasn't sure which were the right words to say in a public setting. The truth is that I had been out of my comfort zone since I was eighteen, so this was nothing new to me. What the Rotary Club lunches did for me was to help me become comfortable with folks who had different backgrounds than me. I was there on my own success, all of which made me interesting. In my years at the club, I never asked for the order, so I never got the order. But what I did get was a tremendous amount of personal growth, which has paid dividends countless times over the years.

> **The truth is that I had been out of my comfort zone since I was eighteen, so this was nothing new to me.**

Telling my story helped me realize that I didn't fit into a box. I had done things that the Princeton boys and girls had never done, and I was okay with that. But in the future, I wouldn't tell my audience everything just because I was asked to.

It soon became clear to me why their motto was "Service above self." One of the great things the club did was to raise a large amount of money during the year, then give it all away by year's end. And I loved being a part of raising the funds. What a great way to give back to the community, something I continue to do today, albeit in different ways now. During the years I was a member, I became a much better contributor to the club when I put service first. I also learned that how you spin your past is just as important as what you should leave out when talking about your past experiences, a lesson that has benefited me many times over the years to follow.

Years later, when people would learn that I held patents and was still striving to acquire more intellectual property rights, they inevitably would say "I got an idea for you to patent, but don't forget to give me my cut when you are rich." Ideas and opinions are easy to find. The trick is finding the one in which it's worth investing your time, your energy, and your money.

In my present-day search for what type of business I wanted to build, I began to tell everyone I knew that I was going to build my own business. When they would say, "Great, what are you going to do?" I would say that I am in the research phase of the build process, then I would ask if they had a suggestion, and I would shut up and listen. You see, there are a few things that I had observed about people, one being they love to tell you what you should do, even if they have no intention of ever doing what they tell you to do. There is a reason why people say "Opinions are like assholes: everyone has one," because they are, and there is no shortage of people willing to share theirs (opinions, that is). So I would take notes, physical and mental notes, of each suggestion offered to me.

One such idea came from my brother-in-law George, who is married to my sister Sue. George told me I needed to find an idea for a product to sell to the electric utility industry. He told me that if I could come up with a product or a service they deemed valuable and that would really work, it could potentially be written into a standard operating procedure, and I would be set for life. After all, the need for electricity was not going away. I can tell you now that I had no idea at the time how great that advice was going to turn out to be. What I can tell you is that I am eternally grateful for George sharing those words. Even if it did not go exactly as he laid it out for me that day, some twenty years later, I see more than he will ever know how valuable that conversation was for my family and me.

CHAPTER TWO
CHANNEL MARKERS

Use the power of thinking positively each day.
Plan for the worst, but expect the best.

When I discovered the book by Norman Vincent Peale, I was floored by his words. I practiced his ideas as a youth with great results, and so it has made me an optimist by nature for life. The negative can and will happen, but I have learned to plan for the worst and expect the best.

Don't tell my audience everything
just because I was asked to.

Telling my story to the Rotary Club helped me realize that I didn't fit into a box. I had done things that the Princeton boys and girls had never done, and I was okay with that. But in the future, I wouldn't tell my audience everything just because I was asked to.

CHAPTER THREE

Thinking Is the Hardest Work There Is

I choose to live by choice, not by chance. To be motivated, not manipulated. To be useful, not used. To make changes, not excuses. To excel, not compete.

—AUTHOR UNKNOWN

Henry Ford once said, "Thinking is the hardest work there is, which is probably the reason so few engage in it." In my way of thinking, truer words may have never been spoken.

As a child growing up in my father's house, I heard him say countless times, "Think, son! Think!" It was his mantra. Everything I did, good or bad, well intentioned or not, those words would sound in my ear constantly for most of my young life. It seemed that nothing I could do was to his satisfaction. And with every effort, the result was always the same—I would fall short of his expectations. If only I would have thought about it, I would not have done what I did wrong, or done it the way I did incorrectly. If only I would have thought about it—before I acted—things would have been more to his liking. All through high school, I tried to please my dad, something I learned years later was not even possible. In his eyes, my lack of thinking was driven home almost on a weekly basis. I know most teenagers believe they can do nothing right in the eyes of their parents, but I was convinced I never would.

Sitting on my perch now, self-reflecting on the island cliff I am so fond of visiting, I realize there were two major lessons I learned all those years ago from my father pounding the words "Think, Son! Think!" into my brain. First, I would never please my father, no matter how hard I tried. Second, I learned to think about everything.

In his own way, he gave me the gift of thought and prethought, which for me is defined as thinking before acting. To this day, I spend days, weeks, months, and in some cases, years, weighing out the choices, the consequences, the what-if scenarios of my forthcoming actions. Don't misunderstand: I take risks and I take chances, and I make fast decisions in business every day. But I also think very hard and very deeply about what it is I am about to do or say. I take calculated risks. I might joke about betting it all on black as in a game of roulette, exaggerating the appearance of being a risk-taker, but only after spending time thinking about the possible outcomes of my actions and understanding the ripple effect based on the information I have beforehand. Being as sure as I can that I am personally able to handle the outcomes of my actions before making them a reality.

Years later, quite by accident, my father paid me a wonderful compliment that I am sure he didn't even realize. In the heat of an argument about something that I cannot remember, he turned to me and blurted out, "Your problem is you think too much!" For me, it was one of life's aha moments.

———————————

Having spent nine years in night school, I learned firsthand what everyone else but me seemed to know: going to college does not by default make you smart. What going to college did for me was teach me how to learn. I now fully understand the need for hard work and determination to complete a task. I need to be wholeheartedly into everything I do if I want to succeed.

> **I need to be wholeheartedly into everything I do if I want to succeed.**

My life and who I was had changed drastically since I had sat in that chair in Mr. Morris's office in the guidance department of high school. Twenty years later, faced with the decision of what to do next, I was bone tired and dreaded the thought of starting yet another career path. After hearing Steve's words, I was forced to reach deep inside once again and decide what I would do going forward. I pulled out a yellow pad and drew a line down the middle of the page to create two columns. At the top of the left column, I wrote, "What I would like to do," and at the top of the right column, I wrote "What I don't want to do." Then I sat back in silence, lit a cigar, and thought about the host of business courses I had taken over the years in my quest to be a college graduate.

In most all those classes, the importance of a business plan was always stressed. In fact, they made me write a business plan so many times that I learned to hate them. It was not that I thought a business plan wasn't valuable, but in my view, they appeared to be based on too much information that was guessed at, with no real, hard proof that the business would work. To me, what most business plans laid out was the "wanting desire" viewed through the "rose-colored glasses" of the writer—the writer wanting more than anything to somehow succeed in business. But there was no clear indication from the plan that the business would ever succeed.

I often thought the professors just wanted to see students struggle with the actual writing of a business plan. And if that was true, then they had succeeded, because writing the plan was harder to me than building the business. Which I later realized was the whole argument true entrepreneurs had when faced with writing a business plan—and why most people couldn't do it effectively. They are too focused on building their business when mental thought is needed. A business must be thought out *first*, and thinking about your business in the form of a plan is going to be some of the hardest work you'll ever do. The principle is simple: the business must be clear in your mind before it can become a successful reality.

With my yellow notepad on the table in front of me, I reflected on the eleven different positions I had held at nine different companies since leaving the army. Every experience I've had deposited in me lessons learned about life and business. By the time I graduated from night school in 1997, I considered myself to have equal amounts of work experience and book smarts. I cannot say I would recommend this path for all, but in the end, it worked for me. What this combination gave me was the confidence that when I would face a challenge in my business, the chances were good that I had lived through it in someone else's business or learned about it in school. (You don't spend time working for other entrepreneurs, building their businesses, and living their dreams without walking away with a great understanding of business practices and life experiences.) I can honestly say that my life up to this day had prepared me for the decision I had to make. I had lived in the trenches and seen the success and failures firsthand. I would not go blindly into the future once I had made my decision to pursue a particular business of my own.

I started writing down business ideas on my yellow pad:

Would like to open a car wash.

Would like to start a limo business.

Would like to start a repair shop.

Would not want to build a trucking company.

Would not want to go back to wall street as a stockbroker.

Would not want to do … *this list grew far longer than I thought it should.*

The only thing I was sure of was that I wanted to build a business. It had to be something I could physically start by myself. It had to have the potential to someday be big. I had to be able to start it on a shoestring budget. I had to be able to do it on the merits of my own talents.

On another sheet of paper, I proceeded to define the pros and cons to each of my "would like" options against my growing list of limiting criteria.

Digging deeper, I thought about what resources I had or that would be available for any of these business options that I was now seriously considering. I contemplated the business-class lessons and the components of a business plan: executive summary, company description, market analyses, organization of management, service or product base, marketing and sales plan, requests for funding, and financial projections. Giving thought to all these components and the details to make them real, I forced myself to look at what I believe are the two most important parts of the plan: start-up costs and funding sources.

First things first. There were two items I would need to secure an answer for if I was to build any of my ideas into a business. Most people start with the market research and the competitive analysis, which are extremely important. But the reality is, if you cannot cover the start-up costs and you do not have a source of funding available, you are pretty much doomed from the start.

Oh, one more thing. And perhaps the most important part of any business plan: find the fatal flaw.

My intent here is not to preach, but if I could give one piece of advice to anyone reading this book and considering building a business, it would be simply this: Find the one piece of the puzzle that could potentially or more seriously be the thing that puts you out of business—this is your business's "fatal flaw." If you cannot define that fatal flaw and address how you will overcome it, you should not go into business.

Think hard about what your business model is! To put it plainly, if your model sucks, then your business sucks, and you go out of business. Just because Grandma makes great cookies, and everyone tells you that you should start a cookie business, you may not be able to build a good enough brand awareness campaign to get anyone to buy them from you. The fatal flaw in the business model needs to be identified and dealt with at the start, or you are doomed to fail.

I know that is a cold slap in the face coming from a guy who lives the power of positive thinking every day. But I also live in the real world, and you have got to have a plan to survive. If you have not addressed the fatal flaw before you get there, you will not know how to get past it when it comes for you. And I can assure you, it will come for you. (I will step off my soap box now.)

My search for what business to build in 2001 had its confirming moment when I focused on the concept presented in my brother-in-law George's box of wonder. George gave me a whole stack of information: magazine clippings, yellow pages of handwritten notes, internet searches, all on ideas and products he had begun to research over the years. Some on products he had sold, considered selling, or just plain thought were really good ideas to someday consider. Turns out George was always on the hunt. I explained to him that I knew nothing about electricity and much less about what it took to make electricity. How was I going to come up with anything of value to sell to an electric utility company?

His response was simple: "Think outside the box."

Buried in the materials from George was information that interested me, because in my mind the idea was surely outside the box: animal mitigation at the substation level. When I investigated this subject, I came across the study published in 1999 by the Edison Electrical Institute in Washington, DC. It stated the second-highest cause of power outages in the United States and Canada was due to small crawling animals such as snakes, squirrels, and raccoons.

When I pushed George on this subject, he gave me three phone numbers to call, which I did. Individuals at three major utilities confirmed that yes, in fact, animal mitigation was a big deal and that utilities spend millions of dollars a year repairing and protecting electrical equipment from the damage of small and crawling animals.

The best part: if I could come up with a solution to prevent this from happening, they would be willing to listen to me.

In further researching the Edison Electrical Institute study published two years earlier, it stated that the highest causes of electrical power outages in the United States and Canada were (1) weather,

(2) small crawling animals, and (3) human error. I was sure I could not change the weather or human errors; both, it seemed to me, were better left for God to fix. I figured it was a sure bet that the electric utility market needed a way to keep animals, specifically small crawling animals, from interacting with equipment and causing power outages. I could not understand how an industry as old as electric production and distribution had not figured out a way to reduce animal-caused power outages. Some will say this find was dumb luck, but for me it was divine intervention.

I began asking questions. What had they done that obviously was not working? What solutions were available? What were the drawbacks of using those solutions? What was the cost to the end user? Did all utilities in the country have the same problem?

The more I questioned the more I started to draw some conclusions. To start, there was no direct 100 percent effective solution available. Most utilities used a variety of options. There were cover-ups, fiberglass wraps installed on specific parts of larger equipment. These cover-ups were designed to prevent animals from touching electrified components of transformers, breakers, or bushings, and taking them to ground by completing the circuit between these energized parts and the steel frames upon which they were installed. There were interior electrically charged barrier systems designed to give the animal a shock as it approached the equipment. There were line guards, fiberglass barrels designed to be installed on overhead lines. As the animal ran along the lines, it would interact with the barrels and slip to the ground, the thought being this would happen before the animal reached the electrical equipment. Unfortunately, all had inherent issues preventing them from being the overall go-to solution for the industry.

Equally as important, I learned what was not working, so I made it my mission to determine exactly what wasn't working. Not so I could copy these alternatives, obviously, but to learn what not to do as I developed a solution. My personal mantra was "Don't solve a problem with a problem!" By learning what had been tried and figuring out what did not work, I identified with the Thomas Edison quote when a reporter asked him if he felt stupid for having failed so many times in trying to invent the battery. He replied, "I have not failed. I've just found 10,000 ways that won't work."

I soon learned the term *animal mitigation* referred to what electric utilities do to mitigate or reduce the animal's ability to interact with electric equipment. Electric utilities have animal issues, both on the lines located on the poles out front of a house and at the substation down the road. The difference is when a squirrel chews through a line on the pole out front, it affects a handful of customers. But when that same squirrel takes a conductor (an energized line) in a substation to ground (a term in the industry meaning *shorting out*), causing the power to go out, the potential is for thousands to be without power. Depending on the severity of the damage, the outage could last for seconds or minutes, and in some cases for days. The electric utility industry in the United States is a regulated industry, which means there are government agencies set up to track and monitor the utility's reliability. This measuring and tracking come down to COMs: customer outage minutes. I tell you all this because it soon became clear to me that if I could develop a solution that worked and kept animals out of electrical equipment, my price would have to be based on the savings offered due to effectiveness, not the material costs. I quickly learned that I was not going to be selling fences or perimeter systems; I was going to be selling increased reliability to the utility industry.

To put this in perspective, there are over three thousand electric utilities in the United States and Canada. The largest one in the US has over 6,600 substations across its territory. Internal studies showed that they had animal problems at some 20 percent of those stations on an annual basis. No matter what matrix you use, when extrapolated across the entire industry, the number of outages and what they cost the industry totals in the billions of dollars per year.

I do not want to imply that all utility companies are the same and spend the same amount of money per year; that is simply not true. What I am attempting to show you is that I found a problem in need of a solution. The industry had a budget and was currently spending countless dollars in an attempt to find a solution that worked.

Keeping my focus on the idea of creating a business designed to keep small crawling animals out of substations sent me on a journey of researching what solutions were currently available on the market and how effective each one was and wasn't. What did they excel at, and where did they fail to meet the customers' expectations? Simple but very important questions that needed answers. I spent a great deal of time designing and redesigning my possible solution. I had learned in one of the many business books I had read that you do not need to reinvent the mouse trap, just build a better mouse trap. Or my favorite: don't reinvent the wheel. I know reading these words sounds very elementary, but it isn't any less true. I always like to say "Life is easy, people make it hard." Never is that truer than in business. In my research, I found a variety of alternative solutions, none of which I thought were a definitive answer to the problem. It also appeared to me none of them were simple, and worse, each had a less than 100 percent effectiveness rating by the industry.

I realized two things: there were enough options available in the market to get a feel for what was *not* working, and there were just enough options that the user had alternative solutions to choose from. But there was no consensus of a perfect solution, confirming what I already believed.

Whether you are determining what business you want to start or have already started one, researching your competition will play a very big part when it comes to marketing. Do you have direct competition, or do you face an alternative solution? To my way of thinking, these are two very different enemies in the business world.

I spent a lot of time in what I call the pre-VANQUISH year, studying animal habits and their actions firsthand. I had borrowed a video camera from a friend and began my journey of learning all there was to know about squirrels, snakes, and raccoons. The joke was that I had spent so much time interacting with squirrels, my wife began to refer to me as "He Who Plays with Squirrels," a veiled reference to a line from the Kevin Costner movie *Dances with Wolves*: "he who dances with wolves." I wore that badge with honor.

While I was very active, this period was also part of what I refer to as my "intentional silence" period; I listened and observed just as much as anything else I did.

I also kept my yellow notepads handy to record my thoughts. Writing out my thoughts was my way of maintaining "intentional silence" while staying extremely busy in my mind. I wasn't ready to promote my business or even solicit any actual sales. It was me determining what my product was going to look like in real life, how I should market it, and what my value proposition was to the industry. This process took the form of a series of details that I needed to address, written on my yellow pad. I drew square boxes next to each idea written on the paper. I figured when I had nailed it, addressed the issue or question to my satisfaction, I would check the box off.

The process of my notetaking included my education on the behavior of the animals—*the problem*; the study of alternative solutions currently available—*the possible competition*; the strong customer base with money primed for a working solution—*the market*. I determined that if I could develop a product to sell as opposed to offering a service, I could someday patent the idea—*potential intellectual property*. All these soon became boxes checked. My idea had the potential to be big—another box checked. I could start with just me being chief cook and bottle washer—box checked. At last, a business that checked all the boxes for what to do and what to build was emerging.

Now I had to address the start-up conversation with my chief investor: my wife, my partner, Christina, who had posed the original question to me, "What will you do?"

Christina and I sat at the kitchen table one evening, as so many couples do when they are about to embark on the path we were heading down, to have "the talk." I was answering Christina's question. "What will you do?"

I had figured out what I wanted to do and how I wanted to do it. I laid out that I would take on three or four or however many part-time jobs needed to help sustain the household during the start-up phase. I explained that I thought we would have to live through a good long five years with no income from the business. She would have to continue to work, and we would keep Ashley and Brandon in their respective schools. We would take student loans, parent PLUS loans, and drain what little money we had in my retirement account. We would not touch her retirement account, but we would stop contributing to it. We would apply for an equity loan on the house. The money from the equity loan would go entirely into the business to cover the start-up costs.

I further explained that once I had a solution worth presenting to the utility industry—since I was virtually unknown to them—the only way I could see one of their decision-makers agreeing to try my solution was if I offered it for free. However, in my experience, when you give something to someone for free, the other party has no real vested interest in evaluating the solution or the product because they have no investment in its success or failure. To overcome this dilemma, I would state that the utility company needed to cover the cost of installation and I would cover the material, thus creating a partnership, in effect. If my solution worked to their satisfaction, I would get to shout it from the mountain tops. If it did not meet expectations, I would take my marbles and go home, so to speak, and we would never talk of my solution again.

> **When you give something ... for free, the other party has ... no investment in its success or failure.**

In making the decision to take the road less traveled, I outlined for myself what I described as my four nonnegotiables. I determined these were necessary for me to address in whatever business I was thinking of or pursuing. My core nonnegotiables include the following:

- In order to succeed with the plan of starting and building my business, I must have strong unwavering support from my spouse.

- Belief in myself and a frank and honest understanding of my own personal abilities and talents, and especially my limitations.

- My business idea had to appeal to my market space, solve a problem, and stand up to the competition directly in my space in the market.

- Recognize, admit to myself, and have a solid understanding of what can put me out of business—immediately. I needed to know my fatal flaw … my kryptonite!

Let me explain.

If you have a spouse, then having the full support of a spouse is the most important part of the equation of success. I mean *unconditional.* It can't be lip service, because if it is, when push comes to shove and what your spouse is really thinking or feeling is not unconditional support, you'll feel like you're caught in no-man's-land. There is a story of a guy who had a very successful business, but his fiancée was despondent because he did not spend Sundays with her and her family. He was too busy working. When he asked another man for advice, the story goes that the second man said, "Which one is easier to replace?"

In retrospect I was confident that Christina had blessed my venture with complete support and understanding from day one. She believed in me and my ability to accomplish the mission I had set out before us. She was confident that I was genuinely in it for the long haul, good or bad, whatever came our way. Not just in words but in actual actions.

I was forty-two years old as I started my business. I had equal parts of formal education and practical business experience. Both good and bad experiences. I believed in myself and my abilities. I had proven to myself that if I didn't know it, I could learn it. And if I was not able to learn it, I could find and pay someone to do it for me. Bottom line: I was confident in what I knew and, more importantly, what I did not know. I was not going to fool myself into thinking I knew it all. I knew my limitations. I knew my strengths. And I was prepared to ask for and get help when needed.

I had found a problem in need of a solution. A problem in an established industry with statistics and money already being spent on solutions that were not working. If I could genuinely offer a solution that worked, I was confident I would be rewarded with some of those existing dollars currently available in my market space. My research showed that there currently was no direct competition. There were other "Band-Aid" alternatives—cover-ups, interior electrified barriers, line guards—but no one was offering what I was going to be supplying: a permanent solution to the problem. If successful, I would be the *only* solution in my space.

Initially, my fatal flaw was my lack of capital, money. I was creating my business completely self-funded. I would be taking an equity loan against our personal residence to start the business. If I was wrong, I stood the chance of losing everything. This was compounded by the second part of my fatal flaw: If a large company (i.e., any one of the multinational giants in the electric utility space) saw merit in what

I was about to present to the industry, they could wake up on any given morning and move into my space, steal my ideas ... and crush me and my efforts. This was a very serious problem, and I needed to formulate a contingency plan.

Looking back, I realize that my lack of funds at the time was a blessing in disguise; I was not going to allocate advertising dollars for my solution simply because I did not have money to spend on it. By default, I would effectively be flying under the radar in my offering; I would be forced to call utilities directly and speak with one individual at a time. My sales pitch would be private, to a degree. There would initially be no education of the potential competition. Even though there was no one in direct competition, I still ran the risk of another vendor already working for the utility in the substation environment who could potentially steal my idea and run with it. I used caution in my approach.

At that point in time, my daughter, Ashley, was about to start her freshman year of college, and my son, Brandon, was a sophomore at a private Catholic high school. Both came with larger-than-life tuition payments. I had to keep my promise to them. I had to make sure they had a chance for an education. After all, that was the goal we, our family, were all working toward. I was desperate to give my kids the opportunity to succeed. Truth be told, I wanted them to make a generational leap in the Moore family line. To be educated, employable, and self-sustaining in a world where it was fast becoming acceptable to stay home on Mom and Dad's couch until you were thirty.

A friend of mine once told me that children of the seventies set out to change the world. Maybe it's just me, but the way I saw it, it was my responsibility to make my little postage stamp of the world a better place. I believed it was my duty to raise children who were respectful, responsible, driven, and productive members of society. And the only way I knew how to do that was to teach my kids old-fashioned morals and values and to afford them the opportunity to get an education so they could accomplish their goals and fulfill their dreams. In doing so, I would achieve my overarching dream of giving back into the world more than I took from it.

I have always had a strong understanding of my time and the value of that time. Even when I worked for others, I felt it was my obligation to give my employers a fair day's work. I hated wasting time and still do. But more important, I always felt that I was paid to do a job and I was going to do it the best way possible.

If I had done my research on the problem properly, then I understood the need and the offering I could bring to the table. My value proposition was defined. In my case, no one knew me. I was not Siemens, Tyco, or GE, so why would they give me a try? I had no history or background to point to. No compelling reason why they should give me a shot. Not a good starting position, I assure you.

Standing there at age forty-two—tying all these personal pressures together like a flour-sack cape and securing it around my neck—I wet my finger, held it up to the wind, and repeated the words that opened this chapter: "I choose to live by choice, not by chance. To be motivated, not manipulated. To be useful, not used. To make changes, not excuses. To excel, not compete."

And with all the courage I could muster, I stood at the edge of the garage roof. Took a deep breath, trusted my cape, and jumped into the abyss, the life of building a business from scratch. I would forever be known from this day forward as an entrepreneur.

CHAPTER THREE
CHANNEL MARKERS

Knowing my fatal flaw—I have to recognize, admit, and have a solid understanding of what can put me out of business—immediately.

I need to know my kryptonite! I need to determine what could defeat my business plan, and just as important, I need to identify a strategy to overcome this when it happens.

Don't solve a problem with a problem.

So many products on the market, especially in my market space, solve one problem only to create two more as a result of the first solution. This is a major no-no when building a start-up company new to the market.

Take educated and calculated risks, not thoughtless risks.

Based on the simple principle of "I should look before I leap" that was taught to me by my mom at a very young age, coupled with the risk/reward calculations of every safety officer I had ever employed—and in keeping with my own survival instincts—I need to think before I don my cape and jump.

I had to have my spouse's strong, unwavering support to start my business.

My spouse needs to be wholeheartedly in tune with, and okay with, the idea that I am going to start a business. The money will be tight, the hours will be long, and there are a whole host of things that can and will go wrong. It is extremely important that my spouse has a clear understanding of what I am about to do and be willing to deal with the pain that will come with starting my own business.

A clear and honest understanding of my personal abilities, talents, and, especially, limitations.

I have to be real with myself. I need to know what I am good at and what I am lacking in. I need to stand in front of the mirror and take a full self-evaluation of my skills, my knowledge, and, most importantly, my limitations. I need to have a strong belief in myself to know that when times get tough, I will know how to seek help.

A business idea that appeals to my market space, solves a problem, and stands up to competition.

This is important! Just because it sounds like a good idea does not make it a good idea. My business has to, from day one, appeal to the market I want to sell to. It has to solve a problem, and it has got to be able to hold its own when compared to a competitor or a competitive product already in the market space. If it doesn't do all three of these things at a minimum, there is a good chance no one will buy what I am selling, and my business will fail.

CHAPTER FOUR

Be There before You Get There

Investment—Those who invest the most in their careers have a greater chance at success than those who don't. Simple? Yes. Do most people invest in their own development to the level of their goals and dreams?

The answer is likely no.

Everyone wants to win, but first, you must make the commitment to what it takes to win—investment.

—*KEVIN EASTMAN, AUTHOR*, WHY THE BEST ARE THE BEST

Let me paint a picture for you in your mind's eye. Just for a moment, imagine yourself having no background in electricity, including how it is generated and distributed. You are standing in front of a room, presenting, trying to convince a group of people employed in a hundred-year-old industry, as big as the country itself, that you have an idea worth listening to. The room is full of mature, educated individuals who have much bigger and what would be perceived as more important problems to solve than what you are presenting a solution to. How would you start to present your case for change and what you think is your new and unique idea to revolutionize the way the world views animal-caused power outages?

If you are like me, the reality of what you want to do has now set in. The great thing about reality is that it causes us to pause and think. Is what I'm thinking of doing *really* what I want to do? If so, what do I need to get clarity on? To plan? To get input from others? Reality takes us from pie-in-the-sky thinking to what is truly possible and what is real. Reality makes us look at the facts and figures, to consider our skills and talents. It helps us to gain the confidence needed to put our plan into action. It also helps us learn what others have done so that we can formulate what we need to do.

In my situation, reality took me completely out of my comfort zone into an industry I knew absolutely nothing about, yet here is where I found a problem in need of a solution. It is said that the best problems to work on when starting a business are the ones nobody else even tries to solve.

My experience up to this point in my life and career had been that if it sounded like a good idea, it was okay to pursue it and hope for the best. My view had now been altered by my decision to start my own business. I was now practicing what Jack Welch referred to as the reality principle. I was facing reality as it is, not as it was or as I wished it to be.

I was focusing on a problem that nobody else was trying to solve to the level I was by investing in myself. I was effectively preparing myself by my actions every day. These actions and investments were formulating the knowledge necessary to build my confidence.

Although I was out of my comfort zone, I was ready, filled with the confidence that I was prepared, because I had invested in myself to the level of my goals. I could not be anything short of successful because I made the commitment to what it took to win. I made the investment.

Here is where the work truly began. I had taken a part-time night job driving tractor trailers from Hershey, Pennsylvania, at the candy plant, to a South Jersey food distribution facility. The facility would break the load down and send it to local 7-Eleven stores and such for consumer sales. I was just the driver, the facilitator. This job was at night and perfect at the time. It paid about fifteen dollars an hour, so I could provide some income for my family and have most of my day to work on my business endeavors.

I backed the tractor trailer into the receiving dock door, as instructed by the guard at the front gate, and walked to the receiving office, as I had done many times. I could tell that the lady behind the glass window was extremely flustered and frustrated. I am sure the driver before me was short with her, as they all seemed to have a reputation of being. I waited patiently at the window with my papers in hand until she acknowledged me. I was polite and respectful and answered each question that she asked. No small talk from me, just the facts.

When our exchange was complete, she looked up at me and said, "You are not like all the other truck drivers."

I replied, "That's because I am not a truck driver. I'm an entrepreneur building a business by day and putting food on the table by night. I am just like you, doing the best I can with what I have today."

Over the years, I have heard so many people tell me "Oh, this is too hard" or "That is too tough." Worse, I would hear them say they deserved better: "I have been working since I was twelve. I am not doing that or working that hard. I don't have to do that; I own the business. I don't work weekends. I don't work nights. I can earn more money on the golf course schmoozing clients than I can working nights and weekends."

I realized that if I am not willing to invest in myself, I will not succeed. There is no secret sauce, no magic potion. What I get out of life will be in direct relation to what I put into it. The result, what I accomplish in both life and business, will be directly affected by my investment in myself, my business, and my career. I understood from a young age what Kevin Eastman referred to in his book when he said "knowledge and confidence come from preparation. Preparation creates knowledge, and knowledge breeds confidence."

One of my favorite business book authors is a man named Jim Collins. In his book *Good to Great*, Collins states, "The direction of a person's efforts is directed by their strategy. That is what will propel you for growth. That is what will move your firm from good to great."

> **Offer the customer respect, service, and a product that I am proud to put my name on.**

A simple lesson to learn and to learn well: my efforts are directed by my strategy.

Simply stated, my strategy for the growth of VANQUISH was this: "Supply a well-thought-out solution, fabricated efficiently from the best materials available, installed to the highest standards, all at the best possible price to the customer." Offer the customer respect, service, and a product that I am proud to put my name on.

From day one, I worked my strategy every day for the first thirteen years, all by myself. Which meant I was on the road, in the field, seven days a week, almost fifty weeks of the year. I spent weeks in Arkansas, Mississippi, and Louisiana in hundred-degree weather. Tracked through the rain and mud daily in North and South Carolina. Sweltered in the Georgia heat, and just for fun battled the massive snowfalls in Milwaukee in January. I know the interstate system in this country like the back of my hand. I knew that if I did not put the time in, make the investment, I would never succeed. I love when people say to me now "You are an overnight success." Yeah, right. Overnight. Ha! A twenty-year overnight success is more like it!

I realize you might criticize me for being away from my family, but I tell you now that when you want to build something as badly and as big as I wanted to, you need to invest your time—for most people, all we have is time. What kept me sane all those early years was my ability to laugh at the fact that if I had ten million dollars to invest, would I have gone into the perimeter fence business? Hell no! The truth is I did not have ten million dollars. I didn't even have a hundred grand to invest when I started. I literally took an equity loan for fifty thousand dollars against my personal residence and stretched it as far as I could. And then rolled that out into the first fence project, which I then gave the finished product away to the largest electric utility in the US just to prove I had something of value to offer. You want to talk about leaving it all on the field, as they say. To my way of thinking and acting, there was no going back! I was here to win, and win big, or fail big trying. The way I saw it, there were no other options for me.

It was a Saturday morning when I pulled our family's copy of the *Webster's Dictionary* off the shelf and sat down at the dining room table in the multipurpose room of our tiny Cape Cod home in Morrisville, Pennsylvania. This room was my study. A place to gather for family meetings. An arts and crafts room for the kids when they were younger. A location for model building and a paint-by-numbers studio. Our family did almost everything at that table located in what was originally a back bedroom when the house was built. But somewhere along the line, a previous owner had knocked down a wall and removed the closet, opening it up to the living room. Now it was filled with Ethan Allen dining room furniture we inherited from my mother-in-law. The size of the furniture was more than the room could handle, but my wife was emotionally attached so, like a smart husband, I tolerated the lack of space.

I opened the dictionary to *W*. I was looking to name the company I was building, and I specifically did not want to call it *Don Moore Fencing*. It was going to be so much more than me someday, and to be honest, my ego was not that big. My rational for choosing a name for the business other than Don Moore Fencing was that I had always believed most people don't take the time to name their business wisely. If you are successful, you will live with that name for a lifetime. So many businesses I see nowadays have names that make no sense regarding what they actually do. I believe that unless you have an unlimited budget for marketing, which will allow you to build brand awareness around your company name, then make the name self-explanatory. I tell people there is a reason my company is not called Don Moore Fencing. When I started the company, I had no intentions of selling it. I still don't, but someday, realistically, I will have to leave it. And whether it stays in the family or not, it should not have to change its name just to stay in business and to be relevant. I have no problem with being proud of your family name, but *Joe's Plumbing* is limited to Joe, in my way of thinking.

I want what I've built to live past me. I want the business to grow and expand its offerings, and as a result, I did not want and still do not want the name of the business to limit my offerings. I see so many companies forced to rebrand themselves to encompass the growth. I believe that when you start, it is hard to know the full scope of what your business will become, so you should not limit your growth by giving it a name that either misrepresents what you do or limits the potential growth. Or worse, has no relevance to what you do every day. Getting a business noticed in the market by potential customers is hard enough; I could not see the logic in making it harder on myself.

For example, there are internet-based companies with names that have little to do with their business, then they run advertisements explaining what they do. Very confusing to me. I don't think a start-up business should take a lot of unnecessary time and energy to educate the customer as they grow the business. My plan was to name my business properly from the start and save myself years of frustration by having to explain what I do repeatedly.

Trust me, I know how great it feels to sit in a meeting at a customer's office and hear the folks say "We have this snake outage problem at substation such and such; what should we do about it?" And the attendees yell, "We should VANQUISH it!" When you hear something like that shouted about your business, it will make your heart skip a beat—I promise you!

A word that started with a *W* was my word of choice because I knew back then that the second generation of my product would have a W-shaped design incorporated in it, and I wanted to capitalize from the start on my future branding potential. Unfortunately, *W* words turned out to be not so exciting or inspirational. I then moved backward in the dictionary because, technically, to my way of thinking, two *Vs* made a *W*. Close enough.

Vanguard was a strong word for sure, but it's used by almost everyone when describing cutting-edge thinking. I surmised that I needed to be more original than that in my thinking. It wasn't long until I had a bingo moment. Working my way through the *V* words, I hit on *vanquish*, defined as "to conquer, to defeat in battle, beat, trounce, rout, triumph over, be victorious over, get the better of; overwhelm, overpower, overthrow, subdue, quell, crush, bring to their knees." To my way of thinking at the time, it doesn't get any more powerful than that!

When Christina walked into the room and asked "What are you looking for in the dictionary?" I replied, "I just identified the most powerful name in the industry—VANQUISH FENCING!"

In the early days of building VANQUISH, I was very passionate about creating a business that was true to my mission and character. I set out to produce a quality product and to provide exceptional service, which by default came from my efforts as the sole employee at the time. Easy to control in the beginning years, but more importantly I knew I needed to set a foundation on which the quality and level of service would be controlled and defined for the future, when it was not just me on the payroll.

I instinctively knew from studying other businesses that they used their branding, the perceived image they portrayed in advertisements, as a starting point. I learned that branding statements appeared to be guideposts or guiding principles that became apparent in a company's products and services as defined by their branding. I realized that the correct image of a company and the services or products it offered were more than just important; they would in fact define the business with their customers from the first moment of introduction. That favorable first impression that we all strive to create. What I originally thought was just clever marketing was in fact a broad array of things combined and categorized under the term *building your brand*. I found that the word *brand* was defined differently than I had originally thought, the mark burned into livestock with a branding iron. A clever logo designed for visual recognition.

As my investment in my education grew, I learned that branding was in fact two things: equal parts of a particular identity or image, regarded as an asset. Versus *branding* defined as "the promotion of a particular product or company by means of advertising and distinctive design."

I looked at companies like McDonald's, Coca-Cola, General Electric, and Apple to see how they used and protected their "brand," and more importantly, their "branding." I realized very quickly that how they were perceived in the market based on their branding was so much more than what they produced or sold into the market, their brand. Intangible versus tangible.

I looked at companies like McDonald's, Coca-Cola, General Electric, and Apple to see how they used and protected their "brand," and more importantly, their "branding."

For example, GE sells an array of products and services using the branding "We Bring Good Things to Life." Coca-Cola, which predominately sold soda at the time, used "Things go better with Coke." McDonald's of the seventies sold hamburgers, french-fries, and milkshakes with fast service using the branding "You deserve a break today." And then you have Apple's "Think different."

My newfound understanding and awareness of how important branding was led me to learn that beginning with marketing—the branding identity—rather than the substance of the offering—the actual brand—can be very dangerous for small companies. It can set the company up to be perceived as overpromising and underdelivering. I made it my personal goal each day to build a physical or substantive brand—the products and services I offered—in a way that I would be proud of until the day I passed the leadership of the company on to the next CEO. I wanted the branding—how I wanted VANQUISH to be perceived in the marketplace—and the brand to be two intertwined yet separate and equal concepts.

In his book *Zero to One*, Peter Thiel makes the argument that a company has a monopoly on its own brand from the start. Realizing this idea years before Mr. Thiel examined the concept, I knew that I needed to concentrate on creating a strong brand in the starting years of VANQUISH. It was so much more powerful to me than just a catchy name or a pretty logo. It was, in essence, about the actual product and service, the physical brand, and by default, my company, all of which would ultimately define the VANQUISH brand and how we interacted with customers and potential customers.

In his book, Thiel goes a step deeper when he talks about building a brand, defining it as follows: "techniques for polishing the surface don't work without a strong underlying substance and real action."[2] It became extremely important to me to build the VANQUISH brand with great care, and my products and service had to be second to none. In order for my branding, my story line, to be believed and accepted by the industry, I needed to first and foremost put forth quality solutions to the industry's problem. I equally needed to identify VANQUISH in the marketplace via its brand—the artwork and marketing phrases

2   Peter Thiel, *Zero to One* (New York: Crown Business, 2014), 52.

used to identify us to the customers and potential customers in my market space.

Thiel also addresses another point that resonated with me. He talks about creating or operating in a monopoly, noting that business should "start small and monopolize." To his point, every start-up business is small at the start, and by comparison, the fact is that every monopoly dominates a large share of its market. Thiel explains that "every startup should start with a very small market."[3] The reason being is that it is easier to dominate a small market than a large one. Start-ups tend to try to sell into an initial market that is too big. And in some cases, this is their fatal flaw.

In my mind, VANQUISH had no choice but to start small. I literally had no money, so I knew that I had to do one substation fence for someone and prove my ideas would work in the real world. I needed to prove that I could solve the problem I identified effectively, repeatedly, with one customer first if I was to ever sell to a second customer. Nevertheless, I created my brand and my branding from day one, because I wanted to define how VANQUISH would be perceived in the market. I wanted control over how my customers would come to know VANQUISH. I wanted my brand and my branding to be clear, concise, representative of my products, and respected in my space from the very beginning. Yes, my brand has evolved over the years, but the foundation and core values have not changed in two decades.

I set forth on this new adventure, now called VANQUISH, with how I began to define the word *courage*: daring to take risks combined with the strength to be compassionate and the wisdom to be humble. My courage is the foundation of my integrity. Integrity is what the VANQUISH brand would stand for from this day forward.

---

3   Thiel, *Zero to One*, 53.

Knowing that I now needed to succinctly state what VANQUISH does, I developed the following vision statement for my fledgling company: "Our vision is to provide barriers that create a safe and secure environment, intimidating to intruders while adding to the overall appearance and protection of assets."

Which I further distilled to what I believe is the most compelling branding statement for my company: "VANQUISH: ALWAYS ON GUARD."

———————————

In the end, I offered my original solution for animal mitigation at the substation level in the form of a test to three major US electric utility companies. I would supply the system, my investment. They would supply the install labor, their investment. Together, we would test it for one year. At the end of which, if it worked, they get to keep the system and I get to shout my success from the mountain tops. In the event that it did not work as I had presented, I would take my system and go away.

Two of the companies wished me well but declined the trial, supporting the opinions of those naysayers who thought I was crazy when I said I was going to build a business around the concept of keeping small crawling animals out of electric utility substations. However, by their declining actions, they further cemented in me the courage I found in the words of David Brinkley when he said "a successful man is one who can lay a firm foundation with the bricks others have thrown at him."[4]

The third, the largest of all, said yes. In so doing, it enabled me to overcome the obstacles of those who said it could not be done. My

4   Public domain quote.

entrepreneurial journey had officially begun. But it definitely would not come easily.

From the vantage of my island cliffside chair, I marvel today at how all the past experiences in my life served me so well in building my business. I know now how important all that comes before prepares us to be there before we get there. Everything we have done is an investment in ourselves for the future, and so, by my logic, it makes sense to invest wholeheartedly today in what you will be come tomorrow. I chose to invest in my own development to the level of my goals and dreams. I have always wanted to win, but first I made the commitment to do what it takes to win.

CHAPTER FOUR
CHANNEL MARKERS

The best problems to work on are often the ones nobody else even tries to solve.

When searching for a business to create and a market to secure for my company's future, it became very clear very early in the process that I needed to be in a niche market. I needed to address a problem most others did not try to solve. This advantage allowed me to operate effectively below the radar for twenty years, which was long enough for me to establish my company as the original thought leader in the industry.

Build your brand from the start.

This is a potential fatal flaw. Once I determined what my product and service were, I needed to decide on two things: (1) how I was going to brand them so that everyone knew what it is that my company did, and (2) what my brand was and how I was going to promote it and protect it. For example, McDonald's brand has always been "good food fast," and its branding back in my day was "you deserve a break today." Two very different items, but the ability to identify a brand and the way it is branded—which can change from time to time—are vital from the start. In my case, how I identified my brand—"VANQUISH, protecting utility assets at the substation level with perimeter fencing systems that prevent small crawling animals from gaining access to a protected area"—and my branding—"VANQUISH: ALWAYS ON GUARD"—would set me apart from my competitors from day one.

My business must have one clear underlying idea for a product or a service, and I must make it or do it the best I possibly can from day one.

I saw so many businesses start out trying to be everything to everyone, in hope of finding something that works. The saying "less is more" is the strategic approach I decided on. My plan was to do one thing great, then do another thing great. I did not try to be a lot of things from the start, because I felt it would dilute my offering if I only did them halfway. I believed that if I focused on one thing, it would be done right and, to my preference, done great from the start!

Don't reinvent the mousetrap; build a better mousetrap.

This statement floated in the syllabus of most of the college classes I took in night school. When I started my company, I researched what the so-called alternative solutions were in the market space I was going to sell into and designed my products and services to improve upon what others did wrong.

Improve on the competition.

Simple, but valuable to follow. I found that I wanted to be in a space where money is being spent on a problem but one where there was no clear winner in solving the problem. That way, if I'm able to supply a product or a service that works, I know companies have already budgeted and spent money; all I needed to do was capture it by improving on what the competition was not doing right.

CHAPTER FIVE

And God Granted Him That Which He Requested

And JABEZ called on the God of Israel, saying, Oh, that thou would bless me indeed, and enlarge my border, and that thine hand might be with me, and that thou wouldest keep me from evil that it may not grieve me! And God granted him that which he requested.

—1 CHRONICLES 4:10

The day came that I knew I had a working business model, and I incorporated my company on December 6, 2004, my son Brandon's seventeenth birthday. Prior to that date, I considered myself to be practicing and building my brand, my product line, my service abilities, and most of all, exposure of my little company with the big solution to animal-caused outages that would inevitably increase reliability for electric utilities in the United States.

I remember many a time telling old-timers in the industry what VANQUISH did: "We keep animals out of substations!" They would laugh and tell me you can't do that. Animals are an act of God, a force of nature. You cannot change nature. I had professors at prestigious colleges and universities tell me that once animals taught their young their migration paths, you could never change their habits. They would say I was wasting my time.

Even though there were days that were tough for me in those early years, I never lost faith. I have always had faith in something greater than me. I chose to identify that as faith in God. From the time I was young, God had always answered my prayers. Even though I knew I had to do my part—invest my time, my energy, my heart in the situation—God always gave me that extra helping hand, that one thing I was missing, and ultimately made the difference between success and failure. This happened for me time and time again, and I began to identify this as divine intervention.

Now, I realize that me being a man of faith and a believer in the power of positive thinking may make it hard for some who read this book to accept this turn in my business as divine intervention, and I would completely accept that; I, too, live in the real world. In my life experiences, miracles and perceived miracles are what happen to other people, never to me directly. I firmly believe that you get what you work for, you get what you invest in, and never does anything come easy. But what I also know is that I have been truly blessed in my life, and when the result of my labor is greater than what I put into it, I give thanks. And that is all I am saying here. When the business started to show signs of sustained life, I was first extremely thankful and energized to work even harder.

My sister Sue, second in line of the five Moore siblings, arrived in this world about a year and a half behind me. We have gone through, as all sisters and brothers do, times of real closeness and times with some distance. With Sue, it was mostly geography that stood between us at any given moment. We always seemed to be on the same spiritual journey, just not always together on timing. We had our own motivations along life's path, but overall, we seemed to consistently be headed toward the same place.

Shortly after making the commitment to start VANQUISH, Sue shared with me, to help maintain my motivation I am sure, a book called *The Prayer of JABEZ*, by Bruce Wilkinson. For those of you who have not read this book, I would recommend you invest the time in experiencing it for yourself. I have been a man of faith since the

> **Being a person of faith does not mean you do not question your faith at times.**

tenth grade, but being a person of faith does not mean you do not question your faith at times. When you are alone and faced with the trials of building a business, you need faith more than ever! At least I did.

I read once that faith is not believing *in* God, faith is believing God. In reading *The Prayer of JABEZ*, I realized that the simple act of asking God for help—"Oh, that thou would bless me indeed, and enlarge my border, and that thine hand might be with me"[5]—was not a sign of weakness. It was not me giving up. It also was not me being greedy or lazy. It was simply me recognizing that there was a power greater than me who, to my way of thinking, had put the stars in the sky. So why would that all-powerful being I called God not help me?

---

5   1 Chronicles 4:10.

I am not writing this to preach, although this would be a perfect time for me to do that. What I am telling you is that having faith in someone or something greater than you does make a difference. I began to pray the prayer of Jabez—specifically the verse I quote above—every morning in those early years. And I can tell you with all confidence, "God granted him [me] that which he [I] requested."[6]

2005 was the year I knew I had a business. I was standing in a substation near Greensboro, North Carolina. It was a gorgeous September morning. The leaves were starting to change color. Bright yellows and deep browns reminded me of the watercolor paintings my wife loves to paint at our kitchen table back home in Pennsylvania. The air had a great cool bite to it, the kind of morning I had always considered a gift from God. The sky was clear, and the sun was full as it made the climb up into the wide-open baby-blue sky.

An installation crew was busy installing a VANQUISH Fencing System at a substation with a history of animal-caused power outages. I could not help but feel good about where I was in life at that moment. Money was still extremely tight. But I had a few sales, and a few sales meant a little revenue, and if I had done my math right, revenue meant profit. I really was taking that moment to thank God for all that he had provided for me. Don't get me wrong—I worked very hard to get to this moment; but I can tell you with full certainty I would not have gotten to that moment without the hand of God and what I call divine intervention.

When my cell phone rang, I looked down at it and I recognized the number: Jerry Allen, the man who had led the team that championed the first VANQUISH Fencing System install in South Carolina.

---

6   1 Chronicles 4:10; emphasis mine: I inserted *me* and *I* to personalize this message.

I find it funny the things that go through your head at a time like that: Do I answer on the first ring? Do I let him leave a message and call him back? Do I try to make him think I am busy? Or do I show him respect and answer immediately? Do I say "Hello, VANQUISH Fencing"? Or "This is Don Moore. How can I help you?" Instead, I answered "Hello, Jerry. How are you on this beautiful morning?"

I genuinely liked Jerry. We had grown to know each other over the weeks it took to install the first VANQUISH Fence System. He would clear his schedule almost every day for a month and have lunch with me. He was what I would describe as a good southern gentleman. He had a beautiful family and a good home life and truly loved what he did for a living. He would eventually retire after having put in what I understood was a good solid forty-six years of service. A trait I respect tremendously, since I had not managed to spend more than 3.2 years at any one thing since I graduated from high school.

As I think back on that moment, I remember how good it was to hear his voice come over the cell phone held to my ear. It's one of those moments in life where the smell of the day or the coolness of the breeze brings my mind's eye back to the feeling of contentment that I felt on that morning when Jerry asked me how many fence systems I thought I could build before the year end. I truly had no idea what I could do. After all, this was all new to me; I hadn't been tested. I had dreamed. I had planned. I had thought about it. But I had never really been asked that question before this moment. I was the sole employee of the company. I used a fabricator in Pennsylvania to make what parts I could not buy. I scraped just enough money together with what little credit I had available to me to do one project at a time. Fabricate it, deliver it, guide the installation, invoice for it, wait sixty days to get paid, and then try to do it again. I had no idea at that moment what I could produce. And so I reached into the air and pulled out the word *five*. "I think I can safely promise you that I could do five more systems before the year is done."

He said, "I'll take them."

It was at that moment both fear and exuberance went to battle deep down inside the pit of my stomach.

Standing there in that substation, that beautiful morning, I truly felt that God was granting me that which I had requested. He was blessing me indeed, and he was enlarging my border, and his hand was with me.

I cannot tell you that at this moment life suddenly got easy or that business just rolled in from here on out, because it did not. In fact, it got harder—a lot harder and a lot more stressful. The point I want to share is that when you start a business, there is a certain level of unknown. A certain level of stress, and some would say the most stress, depending on your reason for starting a business.

In my case, it was the lack of a job coupled with the need to make a living to support life's financial commitments. The desire to be my own boss, to control my own destiny. The dream of building something bigger than me. There was no lack of motivation to try and build a business. The stress was in the unknown. I, like every other entrepreneur, had no crystal ball to look into the future. All I had was my faith. I believed I could do it. And so I proceeded down the path. It was in those days that I became fond of saying "Be careful what you pray for, because you just might get it!"

My stress had now evolved from "How I start a business with nothing?" to "How do I maintain a business with nothing?" How do I meet the commitments I had just made? A totally different kind of stress, but stress just the same.

———————

It was September a year later, in 2006, the year I confirmed I had a business. I was in Kentucky, same type of day, a cool, brisk morning; the leaves were changing again, and I had just finished up the largest system install I had ever done. I once again was feeling proud of myself and my accomplishments. I was driving, headed back toward Pennsylvania, when the phone rang. I looked down at the caller ID as the phone vibrated in the console of the truck. David Hansil's name appeared. I pulled over to the side of the road so that I did not drop the call. David represented a region of substations for what would someday become my largest customer. I remember pulling into this little parking lot in the middle of some small Kentucky town. I remember seeing all the old storefronts decorated for Halloween. They were antique stores set up in what used to be department stores along the main street of town. Stores long ago closed up, displaced by the sprawling shopping malls with their big box anchors located now just outside of town. This was mid-America making its best attempt at revitalizing small-town America.

I was thinking that I would have to bring Christina here someday to visit these shops—she would love it. I remember dreaming of bringing her on these trips and hoping to take a few days to "smell the roses along the way," as they say. I wished that she could be with me to experience the things I experienced daily now that the business was dragging me off to all corners of the country. But as quickly as that dream swelled up in my chest, a voice in my head said this is your dream, not hers. I put the truck in park and answered the call.

David and I had worked together on many a substation that year, and he had just been informed there was some extra money in the budget, and his group wanted to know how many more installs I thought I could do before the year's end. I dug deep inside. I was not as unprepared as I was last year when this call came. My answer was not as enthusiastic as it was last year either. "David, I would be lying if I told you I can do any more this year."

It was beyond my belief to ever think I would have to say those words—to turn down work—but I simply could not do any more with the constraints of completion in the next three months. I was at that moment at max capacity. Talk about a sweet-and-sour moment!

I had booked all that I could do for the calendar year of 2006 and was turning down work. The sad news was I had more work to do, and the good news was I had already committed to all the work I could do for the year. This was the proverbial sweet spot of life, and it felt extremely unrewarding, depressing. But what it confirmed once again for me was that I now had a business, and I had a customer base who could not get enough of what I sold.

In *Good to Great*, Collins states that companies moving from good to great did not focus principally on what to do to become great; they focused equally on what not to do and what to stop doing to become great. I swore that if I had any say, I would not turn down work again and I would be prepared to take all the sales I could get. That simple-sounding action required me to add to the amount of inventory I kept on hand at the end of the year. Which meant I would need more cash to invest in the inventory for my systems.

By my observations, my business had a slow start for the first two quarters of the year. Followed up by a strong second half of the year, when I sold the most systems. The concept of budget-money availability—underspend from other projects released and becoming available later in the calendar year—was something I did not have familiarity with, but I was learning.

Because my product was new to the industry and was slowly becoming acceptable, it would take a few more years for VANQUISH and its solutions to be a budget item for electric utilities. For now, I was regulated to what leftover money could be spent on. Not that I wasn't worth it, or my solutions did not warrant the spend; it was just that, as I learned, these things take time to sort themselves out. I needed to keep working and to be patient. VANQUISH would become a budget line item in due time. At least that is what they told me!

My solution was to take every dollar I could spare and buy raw materials. I had them fabricated and modified and packaged, ready to go in a moment's notice. This not-so-simple change in my business model—going from "made just in time" to "stocked on the shelf, ready to ship tomorrow"—was a philosophy that served me well for almost two years.

The next two years also saw significant growth for VANQUISH Fencing. I was

If there was any doubt I was in business, that doubt subsided.

able to increase production, store inventory, and plan for the work scheduled for 2007 and 2008, while building up a reserve of materials. When the September calls came, I was ready and able to deliver. If there was any doubt I was in business, that doubt subsided.

In 2008, I remember walking into the local Ford dealership and buying my first new dually truck, an F-450 Super Duty, along with two new forty-foot gooseneck trailers. Up until then I was using my family's Ford Expedition with a used twenty-four-foot tow-behind landscape trailer to deliver my system to the job sites. I was moving up in the world of efficiency. Now I could use one trailer to pick up raw materials from my suppliers and one to stage my loads for delivery to the customer's job sites. Business was good!

———————————

In the fall of 2009, my oldest child, my only daughter, Ashley, came to Christina and me and informed us she was ready to get married, and that 2010 would be the year. October, to be exact. We loved her soon-to-be husband, Steve, and we were ready to welcome him into the family with open arms. This would be a celebration like no other, and we were going to have the best wedding I could afford.

But at the end of 2008, the government declared war on the coal industry. What I did not know at the time was that the electric utility industry relies very heavily on coal-fired generation. And when the administration changed its stance on coal, the ripple effects … well, let's just say they shut VANQUISH down. I watched as the orders for my systems dropped. I watched as customer after customer slashed budgets and removed animal mitigation efforts off the table month after month.

When 2009 came to a close, I had lived through one of the worst years in business that I thought I would ever have. Only to be followed by 2010, a year where I did not sell one fence system. The war on coal was in full swing, and VANQUISH was destined to be collateral damage. I kept all this inside. I did not tell Ashley. When this all started, I did my best not to share the facts with Christina either. After all, a mother and daughter planning the wedding of a lifetime; how could I even consider ruining that? Not even for a moment.

By the time the night of October 30, 2010, was over and the bride and groom had left the reception for the night, my wife turned to me and said we should tip the waitstaff because they had done a wonderful job. I looked her right in the eyes and said, "Honey, if we do that, we will be walking home. I have thirty dollars in my pocket and three hundred in the checking account, and after that, we are broke."

In the first decade of VANQUISH, I was a one-man band, the only employee, literally. I will be the first to tell you that although I was the only employee, I was not alone. My understanding of divine intervention gave me a sense of not being alone—ever. The utility company would purchase my solution, then hire an installation crew, whom I would teach, one on one, on site, how to properly install my fence system. This process meant I would make the cold call, make the presentation, and close the sale to sell the system. Then I would switch hats and contract the fabricator to make my proprietary components. Components I had designed. Then I would put on my purchasing hat and set out to buy all the non-proprietary parts needed to support my solutions in the field installation. Switching to my logistics role, I would collect all materials and load them on a truck, a trailer, the back of my 2000 Ford Expedition, or whatever was available, depending on the size of the sale and the distance from my rented garage in Bristol, Pennsylvania.

I often thought of myself as the guy I remembered seeing on *The Ed Sullivan Show* when I was a young boy spending the night at my grandparents' house. The man would come out on stage and set up a series of poles, on top of which he would set plates to spinning. In some cases, he would have multiple plates all spinning at one time. The trick was to go from pole to pole, plate to plate, and keep them all spinning. I was the real-life version of the plate spinner. As you can imagine, this was not only physically exhausting; it was mentally draining as well. But in all honesty, I would have told you then—and now—I enjoyed every moment. I was living my dream. Building my business. I was tired but a good tired.

It has been said that if you do something you love, you will never work a day in your life. I believe I was and am today living proof of that. I love what I do!

Who would have thought I could build a business on a national level by preventing squirrels from entering electric utility substations! If it was not for divine intervention, I am not sure I would have pursued my dream, and I am sure it would not have been to keep small crawling animals out of electric utility substations.

CHAPTER FIVE
CHANNEL MARKERS

Don't settle for good; strive for great in all that I do.

This rule was inspired by Jim Collins, after I read his argument that good is the enemy of great—simply because it is too easy to settle for good.

Keep the company lean and flexible.

I knew that because of a lack of capital, I was going to have a lean company from the start. I also knew that when it was just me on the payroll, I could be flexible. As I grew the business and the cash flow, the money became a little easier to come by. I always ran the fear of adding too many people, which would affect cash flow and limit my ability to stay flexible.

Work in the three dimensions of success: (1) learn from the past; (2) produce in the present; (3) prepare for the future.

In the process of building a business, especially one from nothing, I found that I needed to maintain a focus on what was really important. I needed to learn from the past experiences. I needed to manufacture or produce in the present, while continually preparing for the future of my company. This rule is universal for any stage of the build that I am in.

Reward yourself when you accomplish major milestones.

I had a boss once who taught me that when I had a great success in business, I should reward myself. Go to dinner, have a drink, buy a car, build a house, enjoy a bottle of wine—do something to reward yourself. For two reasons: (1) so that you remember the win when things don't go your way; (2) so that you will entice yourself to desire the win again by accomplishing another of your major milestones.

Face reality as it is, not as it was or as I wish it were.

This rule was also inspired by Jack Welch and my dad. Both men harped on living in the reality of things. My dad would say, "Don't feel sorry for yourself, son; get up, face reality, deal with it." I have now and forever adapted that attitude in life and in business. I cannot make choices for my business based on what I would like to see in the real world. I need to make choices on what I know to be real in the world today.

CHAPTER SIX

There Is No Safety Net

I've missed more than 900 shots in my career. I've lost almost 300 games. 26 times, I've been trusted to take the game winning shot and missed. I've failed over and over and over again in my life. And that is why I succeed.

—MICHAEL JORDAN

In the beginning, as a newly minted entrepreneur, I believed that building a business reflected who I was as a person and was directly tied to my want, my need, to be successful. Which by that logic meant that failure should be a direct reflection on me and my abilities: If I fail, I should be forever labeled a failure. The reality is I should not be labeled a failure.

I stood at that moment when failure was a very real and a very strong possibility. VANQUISH had been in business for ten years at this point. As a country, we were in one of the longest and worst recoveries of the economy of all times. It took all I had to continue daily when I truly saw no way forward for VANQUISH. To my way of thinking, if the government continued along the path of eliminating coal-fired generation—the cost of which, the news reported, would be staggering—I had to wonder if there would ever be money in the electric utility's budget for animal mitigation.

I am all for saving the planet as much as the next person, but this was in my backyard; it was real for me, not just an issue on a ballot somewhere. What I had worked for and built every day of my life for the last ten years was being jeopardized. This dilemma was as real as it could get for me. After ten years in business, I would not say I was complacent, but I would say I thought I was comfortable, that I was in a place where I could survive almost anything. I could not have been more wrong.

As I took stock of where I was, both financially and as a person, I searched deep inside and remembered the values I hold dear. "If it is meant to be, it's up to me" kept coming back to mind over and over. I recalled my burn-the-boat philosophy. There was no turning back, only taking steps forward. If it doesn't kill you, it makes you stronger. My faith, I held tight to it. I had to continue with the same determination with which I had started VANQUISH all those years ago.

The one big difference I kept coming back to was that I had already built a brand. I had built a system, a solution that worked. I needed to stay strong, to pick up the pieces. Trust in God and keep on marching. I wish I could tell you that I had a magic pill or a secret spell that fixed everything. I cannot. What I can tell you is I went back to work. As a coach would say, back to the fundamentals. I called all my customers and pushed all my contacts. I asked questions. I stayed fresh in their minds. I worked hard to keep myself focused, just as I had done back on day one. I prayed every morning.

In his book, *What It Takes: Lessons in the Pursuit of Excellence*, Stephen Schwarzman, the chairman, CEO, and cofounder of the firm Blackstone, says[7]

> every entrepreneur knows the feeling: that moment of despair when the only thing you are aware of is the giant gap between where you find yourself and the life and business you imagine. Once you succeed, people see only the success. If you fail, they see only the failure. Rarely do they see the turning points that could have taken you in a completely different direction. But it's at these inflection points that the most important lessons in business and life are learned.

I was once again at one of those reflection points described as facing the gap between what is and what I had imagined. Not to get political here, because as my daughter tells me, if I speak politics in this book, I run the risk of offending half the population of potential readers. So I will simply say that the next election cycle seemed to turn the tide in my favor as a business, and the war on coal seemed to subside a bit. And that fast, the greatest thing started to happen. Customers started asking for quotes and proposals, and out of what was one of the most potentially dark spots came a renewed interest in what I had to offer.

———

I had rented a small shop building in Bristol, Pennsylvania, a couple of years earlier from a man named Robert Katzmar. The shop was located about a fifteen-minute drive from my house. Bob, as I called him, treated me like family. He encouraged me at every turn. He had owned his own business for years and believed very strongly that

---

7   Stephen A. Schwarzman, *What It Takes* (New York City: Avid Reader Press, 2019).

everyone should work for themselves at one point or another in their life, if for no other reason than to learn what it takes to make a payroll. Bob would eventually become one of my closest friends, and to this day, when time allows, we ride motorcycles together along the winding roads that form the Delaware River Valley between Pennsylvania and New Jersey. We also enjoy a good cup of coffee while sharing stories and past adventures over breakfast on Saturday mornings from time to time.

In those days, I got up each morning and went to work at the rented shop. No one knew there was no work at the shop; they just knew I was doing what I had always done. I had originally built my business one step, one call, one task at a time. As my drill sergeant in basic training was fond of yelling, "By the numbers, trainee. By the numbers! Do it again and again if necessary. But get it right! Your life depends on it."

He was right … my life did depend on it. I had no alternatives. I had to take every step one at a time, just as I had done in the beginning. It worked once, and it would work again—it had to work again.

> **I was learning a lesson that would pay dividends in the years to come.**

I was learning a lesson that would pay dividends in the years to come : no matter how long you are in business, you will constantly and repeatedly have to go back to the basics. Be prepared for it. Don't let it scare you into giving up. Just because something doesn't work out as you had originally planned, that does not make you a failure. I have learned that it is not how many times you fall; it is how many times you get back up.

I also realized something significant during this time. Although I believed the outside forces over the preceding eighteen months were very strongly stacked against me, I did not let the fear of failing stop me. Yes, my inner fear of not accomplishing what I had set out to accomplish was overwhelming, especially after having been in business for over ten years. I was determined that it would not be my undoing.

I've read that almost half of all start-ups fail in the first five years of business. Which by my math says that if you can stay in business past the five-year mark, your chances of being in business for ten years are greater. Therefore, if you can stay in business past the ten-year mark, you have a greater chance to make it to fifteen years. As I write this, I realize how silly that sounds. But at the time it was a yard stick I used to measure my success. So here I was, over ten years in business ... great! But a closer look said I had just gone through a tough time that would give the average person justifiable cause for concern—and perhaps even cause them to quit. Not to mention the bank, the creditors, and the suppliers that were lined up. Yes, I was concerned, but afraid, circumspect to fear? No. I believed in me! As Winston Churchill once said, "Success is the ability to go from failure to failure without losing your enthusiasm."

About a month after Ashley and Steve's wedding, I received an order for a fence system. It wasn't a big job, but it was a job just the same. It may not sound like much, but it renewed my resolve. It gave me hope. This job, this sale, this project was like the first sprout of a crocus, a spring flower pushing through the ground while the remnants of the winter frost still lay all around it.

The first project in a year and a half made the year-end holidays joyous. There truly was a cause for celebration. I had spent the last eighteen months struggling with the loss of *all* revenue and had considered taking on part time jobs again just to make it through this period. Compounding this fact, I had decided to keep the lack of revenue from my family as best I could.

Hope truly does spring eternal!

My basic approach to life: Wisdom does not come by accident. It does, however, come by experience. I believe we need to pursue wisdom with all our hearts to grow as individuals, as leaders, and in our businesses. Wisdom, to me, is the product, the end result of learning the right or the wrong way to do something. A gentleman named Larry Vise, who gave me many words of wit over the years, once said, "You received your first 'PhD' at VANQUISH."

At first glance, the joke was that I literally received my first "post-hole digger" as a fence man at VANQUISH. But the deeper meaning hit me just as strongly in his words: "What you learn by owning and building a business is considered by many to be a doctorate-degree-equivalent in education from experiences lived." Meaning if you count the costs of the mistakes you have made and will make in business—especially your own business—the cost will equal the price paid not only in real dollars but in time invested by most doctoral candidates who achieve the educational goal of obtaining a PhD.

Today I use this phrase when my team is tempted to share hard-earned secrets with customers or competitors. I remind them that I paid for that education that they are so willing to share. I tell them that knowledge came at a steep cost, and we are not giving it away to those who did not pay for it or at the very least earned the right to the knowledge.

To me, wisdom is earned. In most cases, by reading, learning, firsthand experiences (a nice way of saying *mistakes*, in my mind), and in some cases through corrective criticism.

I was introduced to the term *corrective criticism* in the tenth grade of high school when my mechanical drawing teacher introduced me to his red pen. My drawings came back looking like someone had cut themselves shaving while leaning over them. Red lines everywhere. He told me his critics were just that—corrective criticisms—and that I should view them as learning experiences and notes to show me ways to improve.

I can tell you now that even though it did not help my self-esteem, my teacher taught me, at a very young age, to be more comfortable receiving input from others whose objectives were to make me better. Whose motives were focused on teaching me alternative ways to look at things.

It was in these early years of learning, of being teachable, that the basis for my love of learning was formed. I soon realized that as smart as I thought I was, there was so much I did not know. It is in those drawing classes that I began to grow my love for learning new things, new thought processes, and new ways of looking at information. Most of all, those classes taught me to research accepted practices in a particular industry before assuming I knew something. But that is a story for a whole other book.

I began to learn the language of corrective criticism, so to speak. I have found that through the years, prior to owning my own business and more so in the years I have been in business, the better I became at listening—really listening to what was being taught, the corrective criticisms—the smarter I got. The more I practiced listening and learning, the more I found that there was no end to people who were willing to help me, guide me, teach me. I firmly believe in the words credited to Buddha: "When the student is ready, the teacher will appear." I understand today that Buddha may not have actually said those words, but it does not make them any less meaningful for me.

Conversely, I also noticed that those who did not want to listen, those who wanted to debate every suggestion, tended to miss the lesson being offered in the moment. I am reminded of a quote my sixth-grade teacher wrote on the board for us to ponder: "When I was a boy of fourteen, my father was so ignorant I could hardly stand to have the old man around. But when I got to be twenty-one, I was astonished at how much he had learned in seven years." He attributed these words to Mark Twain at the time. I have also come to learn that Mr. Twain may have never actually spoken those words, but again it does not make them any less true for me. We truly can learn, and in that process, we will surely come to learn that those offering corrective criticism may just actually have knowledge worth learning.

I realized long ago that being teachable is not about competence and mental capacity; it's about my attitude in any given situation. I learned to have the desire to listen, to learn, and to apply what was shared with me. I developed a hunger to learn, to discover, and ultimately to grow. I fostered in myself a willingness to be taught, to learn new ways, and to unlearn old ways, and, if necessary, relearn the lessons I may have missed the first hundred times I tried.

Mark Twain puts it this way: It ain't what you don't know that gets you into trouble. It's what you know for sure that just ain't so that gets you into the most trouble.[8]

All the great books on business had told me that for any business to grow, you must develop a team. An entrepreneur can surely create something from nothing, but they cannot build it to any great size without the addition of people. Preferably good people with good ideas who are willing to join you in your endeavors. I like to say

8   Matt Seybold, "The Apocryphal Twain: 'Things We Know That Just Ain't So," published October 6, 2016, https://marktwainstudies.com/the-apocryphal-twain-things-we-know-that-just-aint-so/.

"People who are willing to play in your sand box and work to make your dream come true."

I have always talked about VANQUISH in terms of "We." *We* did this, and *we* did that. *We* are proceeding in this direction with this product. I was the only employee of VANQUISH for the first thirteen years, yet I would stand in front of a room full of engineers at an electric utility company and give my presentation, all the while referring to my team of designers, fabricators, researchers, and such. I would tell how we were all working to provide the best solutions, the best service money could buy when it came to animal mitigation. I knew someday I would have a team behind me; of this there was no doubt. Years later people would ask me, "How could you have come across so sincerely in those presentations?" My answer, jokingly, was to quote the character George Costanza from the show *Seinfeld*: "It's not a lie if you believe it."

Now, I am not suggesting that you lie to get business. I am suggesting that you must believe in yourself in order to sell other people on your idea or, more importantly, to join your team. Never underestimate the need for passion in your presentations. Never think small. Always think big. Always describe where you are going and what that looks like. *Be there in your mind before you get there in person.* I could see my fabrication facilities. I could see my warehouses. I could see my delivery trucks. I could see my install crews. I could see it all, every step of the way. I spoke them all into existence every day. I truly had faith in God, and I believed in myself and my abilities to make my dream a reality. Was it easy? No way! But the more I thought it through and the more I visualized my success, the easier it got.

It is said you need to expect your success before it can happen. I believe that is true. I *knew* I would be successful. To my way of thinking, there were only two possible outcomes: success or failure.

Neither one was the end. If I was successful, that would surely lead to more success. And if I failed, well that, too, would eventually lead to success. Failure is only a moment in time along the road to inevitable success. I am only a failure if I stop trying.

In the years since I made the first phone call to gauge the interest in a solution for animal mitigation at the substation level, I had created a stand-alone business that had no direct competitors. There were alternative solutions, but no industry-leading solutions until I created one in the product offerings of VANQUISH. We offered 100 percent success. At every station in which a VANQUISH system had been installed, there were no more recorded animal-caused outages. No other solution could say that.

By January of 2013, VANQUISH was back in growth mode. Opportunities were coming in daily. I was working with customers in other regions of the country. I had successfully modified the design of my products, and now I had thirteen years of 100 percent success in reducing animal-caused power outages. I had also added a fence system to the VANQUISH offerings that successfully contributed to the reduction of copper theft in substations.

VANQUISH and I were thought of by the industry as true solutions providers. Customers started to bring me out-of-the-box problems to see if I could design a solution for their specific needs. Business was good! So good that I decided I needed a better base of operations in the Charlotte, North Carolina, area.

Duke Energy had recently merged with Progress Energy, and I believed this could only be good for me in the future. One was a very good customer, and the other not so much. Being an eternal optimist, I could only see the one influencing the other in my favor. After all,

I never once thought that I couldn't sell to every electric utility in the country; it was just that I was only one person and I only had so many hours in a day. So Christina and I went industrial building shopping.

Christina traveled down from Pennsylvania, and we put a circle on the map and found a real estate agent to take us around. Having never purchased commercial real estate before, I quickly learned it is a whole other ball game from residential purchases. Questions we needed to define included the following: Do we need office space or warehouse space? A laydown yard for materials or truck parking? Would I someday want to fabricate my own components, and if so, would I be better to get shop space now or later? Decisions, decisions … way more than I thought when I said "Let's get a Realtor."

After much research, we landed on a location on the border of two towns, Kannapolis and Landis, about forty-five minutes north of Charlotte. A small plot of land with a two-bay shop, a shed-type warehouse space, and a small office building. Perfect! I took extreme pride in knowing that I had found a facility within my budget that would accomplish all my needs in a facility. In March 2013, VANQUISH planted a flag and set up shop in the great state of North Carolina.

What I needed was someone on the team who understood what the strategy of VANQUISH was and to assist in implementing that strategy.

When I closed on the property, I knew that I would soon start my search for what would be my first employee, whose job it would be to help me carry out my strategy. That person would not be hired to install the product; they would not be hired to make the product; they would not be hired to design or invent the product.

They would be hired to help me accomplish the implementation of my strategy. I believed very strongly that we could hire fabricators, we could hire install crews, we could source good materials. What I needed was someone on the team who understood what the strategy of VANQUISH was and to assist in implementing that strategy. Together, we would become a team—a "we."

Andrew Carnegie is said to have described teamwork as the ability to work together toward a common vision. The ability to direct individual accomplishments toward organizational objectives. It is the fuel that allows common people to attain uncommon results. I wholeheartedly believe this is true and I strive to lead my team to follow this common vision every day, to this day.

When Scott Reeder, who would be the first VANQUISH employee, agreed to leave his job at the local gun store and join what would become the start of the VANQUISH team, I told him the story of the Viking warlord who had sailed across the waters to a foreign land. On the shore, he gathered his army and brought in his generals to give his motivational speech. To convince them to fight for his cause to take new ground to expand the empire. To impart words of wisdom, as all good team leaders do with their team. To lay out clearly his strategy. To win their respect, their loyalty, their undying love, and desire to accomplish the mission.

As the Viking warlord came to finish his speech, he turned to his generals and instructed them to "burn the boats." The generals looked at their leader with utter confusion. Burn the boats? Are you out of your mind? What if we are defeated today and need to retreat? Without the boats we have no exit strategy. No fallback position. It is said that the leader stated simply and clearly: Today we fight to win. We put all we have into the process, and either we win or we die trying, but we do not retreat. There is no going back. We came here today to win, and that is what we shall do.

I concluded the telling of that story to Scott and each new member of the VANQUISH team in turn by saying "You do not need to have my passion to work at VANQUISH. You just need to understand my passion. I am here to win. I have personally burned my boat."

I have since told that story to every new hire when they made the decision to join the "we" that makes VANQUISH great!

One Christmas, Scott and the team presented me with a picture of a burning Viking ship framed and signed by all the members of the VANQUISH team at the time. It now hangs proudly on my office wall in the VANQUISH building in North Carolina, serving as a reminder to me and all who see it. *We* need to win because, together, *we* have burned the boats.

According to a 2013 study done by one of my largest customers on the costs versus the success rate, the VANQUISH system was the best investment. The study showed that over a ten-year period, cover-ups were the least expensive solution but were only about 50 percent successful. Interior fences with electrically charged barriers cost more, but only returned an 80 percent success rate. VANQUISH, being the most expensive alternative, was 100 percent successful for ten years running. Their conclusion: an ROI (return on investment) was worth pursuing whenever possible.

As an aside, this study was reenforced by a follow-up study done in 2018 that once again confirmed that every dollar spent on a VANQUISH Animal Deterrent System was more than paid for by the cost savings of experiencing fewer animal-caused outages and increased reliability in the reduction of recorded COMs (customer outage minutes) annually.

When I first started in the financial markets as a stockbroker working for a high school friend, Roger Hicks at Prudential Securities, he taught me that when you have a success in your business, you need to reward yourself. In the world of "Great job! Now, what will you do next?" he said it is necessary to take a moment, celebrate your success, go to dinner, take a trip, or buy yourself something to mark the occasion so that when things don't go so well you can look back and remember what success feels like. So I bought a truck. A 2013 black-on-black four-door Ford F-350 Platinum edition pickup, with all the bells and whistles, to reward myself. I am convinced that truck thinks it is a sports car at heart. I love that truck!

By the time 2013 ended, I had grown the company from one employee, me, to twenty-eight people and over $2.5 million in equipment, with gross sales topping $8 million. Who would have believed that would even be possible back in 2001, when Steve came into my office and told me to dust off my résumé? Who would have believed it, when I had thirty dollars to my name at the end of my daughter's wedding? I would ... that's who. Only me. I tell you with confidence: you must believe in yourself, and you have to be willing to stay the course; even when times get rough, you will have a fighting chance. If you are willing to sacrifice, work hard, think it through, execute, then repeat repeatedly, I am confident that you, too, can make it work for you and your business. You have to find a way to continue.

Through the words of Theodore Roosevelt in his "The Man in the Arena" speech, I found strength and ultimately modified my original belief system concerning failing. I am not ultimately labeled a failure because I fail. Failing does not make me forever a failure if I learn from it; it makes me wiser.

The Man in the Arena[9]

It is not the critic who counts; not the man who points out how the strong man stumbles, or where the doer of deeds could have done them better. The credit belongs to the man who is actually in the arena, whose face is marred by dust and sweat and blood; who strives valiantly; who errs, who comes short again and again, because there is no effort without error and shortcoming; but who does actually strive to do the deeds; who knows great enthusiasms, the great devotions; who spends himself in a worthy cause; who at the best knows in the end the triumph of high achievement, and who at the worst, if he fails, at least fails while daring greatly, so that his place shall never be with those cold and timid souls who neither know victory nor defeat.

This speech has been framed and hung on the wall in my office located in the VANQUISH building of North Carolina, enabling me a reaffirming read every day. This reaffirming is what allows me to rise each morning before the sun and attack the day with the same overpowering energy and anticipation as a young child on Christmas morning, day after day, no matter what the previous day left me with.

---

9   Theodore Roosevelt, "The Man in the Arena," Transcript of speech delivered at the Sorbonne April 23, 1910, https://www.theodorerooseveltcenter.org/Learn-About-TR/TR-Encyclopedia/Culture-and-Society/Man-in-the-Arena.aspx.

Remember, I am just an average guy of average means, who put my heart in it and threw myself off the roof. As Michael Jordan's quote that opens this chapter reveals it is the act of trying over and over again that breeds success. I flew because I didn't know I couldn't fly. Which is why I can say to you today with all humility and confidence, "Always trust your cape!"

CHAPTER SIX CHANNEL MARKERS

I am not a failure if I do not reach my intended goal.

Although I strive every day to succeed, I must remember that if I fail today, it does not make me a failure. VANQUISH and I are only declared failures when we give up and stop trying.

Invest in my research.

Pretty self-explanatory, yet I found I needed to remind myself to invest back a portion of my earnings, especially in the early years when money was the tightest. I found I needed to continually learn new ways and to develop improvements based on the results of my research.

Invest in myself.

As the only employee in the beginning, I needed to invest in myself. Which, the truth be told, even after twenty years, I still need to invest in myself. I need continual education on processes, products, and people, what I called the three *P*s of my business.

Invest in my business.

It would be nice if I made one investment, started the business, and then just sat back and reaped the rewards of that investment. Unfortunately, it doesn't work like that. I needed to make a commitment to reinvest my time and money if I wanted my business to grow past the point of just making a living for myself. I looked at my business as a living, breathing life form, and it needed to be fed so it could grow into a more productive organization and a more dynamic member of my marketplace. I wanted, I needed, VANQUISH to be a self-sustaining entity someday, and that required an investment to be made every day.

Learn the language of corrective criticism, and develop a hunger for the process.

My mechanical drawing teacher in high school taught me the value of corrective criticism when he marked my drawings with his red pen for the first time. He made me realize that the only way to learn, to improve my production, is to see where I am deficient. Most times, that comes from someone criticizing my actions, my plan, my ideas. The trick is to not take it personally. To listen to the opposing thoughts being presented, evaluate them, incorporate them, or discard them as I see fit. I learned to listen to the language of corrective criticism.

Learn to listen.

This is one I struggle with to this day. I know I should listen more, but I find myself always talking, and when I am doing that, I am not learning. Listening keeps me humble. It also helps me to learn. It improves my relationships with my employees and my customers. By truly listening, I understand what others need from me, and that affords me the opportunity to grow the business.

Be teachable.

Being teachable goes hand in hand with corrective criticism. Mr. Raymond Cox instilled these words in me. He convinced me that I had to "always want to learn." Learn how to run a paper route, work at a hardware store, stack lumber on a truck, repair bicycles as a kid.

Years later, learn how to drive a truck, trade stocks on Wall Street, develop a financial plan. Being teachable is instinct for some, but for me, I believe I had to develop it within myself.

Embrace the learning process.

Education is key to success. Recognizing what I don't know is the first step in the learning process. It is equally important for me to understand what I am missing in my thought process as it is for me to effectively search it out and educate myself. In today's environment, education abounds, and all we have to do is seek to learn by embracing the learning process.

PHOTO GALLERY

Donald E. Moore, CEO and founder of VANQUISH *Fencing*

Incorporated

Don surveying a job well done!

VANQUISH *ANDERSON* Model

VANQUISH *APHRODITE* Model

VANQUISH *DEMETER Model*

VANQUISH *ANDERSON Model*

VANQUISH *HESTIA Model*

VANQUISH *WILSON Model*

VANQUISH *Facility 2013/2014*

VANQUISH *Facilities 2022*

Don, Christina, Ashley, and Brandon

Don, Sophia, Madelyn, and Christina

Don, Christina, Madelyn, Ashley, Sophia, Stephen, and Brandon

Don Living the Dream!

Sophia, Madelyn, and Poppy

CHAPTER SEVEN

If There Is No Competition, There Is No Progress

....

You can't connect the dots looking forward; you can only connect them looking backwards. So, you have to trust that the dots will somehow connect in your future.

—*STEVE JOBS*

I am and always have been an early riser. I live by the mantra my grandmother taught me all those years ago, "Early to bed, early to rise, makes a man healthy, wealthy, and wise." Couple that with an entrepreneurial mindset: when I was in middle school, I wanted more than anything to have a paper route. My own business. Earn my own money. Have my financial independence.

In Hopewell, that meant you either delivered the afternoon papers—the *Trenton Times* or the *Philadelphia Bulletin*—or you got up each morning before dawn and delivered the *Trentonian*.

My friend, Keith Wykoff, two years my senior, born in Hopewell, not a transplant like me, had claim to the two after-school routes. They had been handed down to him by his older brother, and in time he would hand them down to his younger brother. So by default, I got the morning run. "The *Trentonian*, On the Doorstep by Six O'Clock" was the slogan at the time, and so I was up and out the door on my bike, folding and throwing papers across the town before the morning sunrise.

> **I feel sincerely sorry for kids today; there is no chance they will ever know the pure satisfaction of managing a paper route.**

Little did I know at the time, but that paper route, and the three years that I had it, would teach me some of the most important lessons about life and business that I would ever come to know. When I look back now, I feel sincerely sorry for kids today; there is no chance they will ever know the pure satisfaction of managing a paper route. Unlimited production quantity: they would print as much as you could sell. Protected territory: the neighborhood was your field to farm. Fixed pricing: it was set for you, and all the world knew it. No chance for you to be undercut on price. Service was your chance to shine—on the porch before six, dry, and in a plastic bag when it rained or snowed. And just for fun, Mother Nature would do everything in her power to make your morning difficult enough for you to appreciate the beautiful mornings when they came your way. The best part in those days: people appreciated good service, and good service almost always guaranteed a good tip come collection day.

I am confident I did not invent the tactic, but I am sure I worked it to perfection. In those days you would tell your district manager how many papers you wanted bundled and dropped at your front door each morning. He would give you a bill, and twice a month you paid him for the papers you bought. It was up to you to sell them. He really did not care who you sold them to, as long as you paid for what you got. I always ordered twelve more papers than I needed. Along the route each morning, I would single out twelve new potential customers and deliver them a paper for a week, free. On Friday night, I would stop by and ask how they liked the paper and the service. Then I would invite them to become a customer. Not all but most would agree and give it a shot. The secret was they could go buy the paper at the corner store, but I made it easy … right on the door mat each morning before 6:00 a.m. Service sells!

I had my route down. I continually worked the delivery route to its most efficient run of my time, being careful to run the down hills to my advantage, since I was pedaling the whole time. I had outfitted my "paper bike," which was different from my ten-speed riding bike, with an oversized front handlebar basket and two saddle bag baskets in the rear. I also outfitted myself with two over-the-shoulder canvas bags, one on each side of my body. I would work on my front porch to fold and fill all the bags and baskets before I left the house. The large basket on the handlebars extended out over the front tire; there, I would place a few flat papers under the folded ones and hold them down with a rubber strap.

Each morning, as I neared the end of my route, I would time it so I would be in front of the Baptist Church on Broad Street, just as the "New York bus" was loading the daily commuters headed into New York City to their skyscraper offices.

"Papers here! Get the *Trentonian*. Get your paper! Enjoy the ride while you catch up on the news!"

After a couple of weeks of priming the pump, I was selling on average thirty-five flat papers out of the basket on my handlebars to people, not as a household on my route but a customer and a sale just the same. I had my own mobile paper stand. I did not have to get off my bike; I just stood there with it braced between my legs, collecting the money. I remember giving the bus driver a free paper for helping me by waiting just a second or two more for me to finish up my business. The beauty of this was it was cash money and, in most cases, a good tip to boot … every morning!

One day, a new district manager asked me how I was growing my route and my sales in a small sleepy town like Hopewell, when most paper boys in his district were losing customers. I was proud of my accomplishments, and so I told him what I have just told you. Next thing I know, he is giving me a list of houses along my route to give a free paper to for a week, and lo and behold, a paper box shows up on the pole out front of the Baptist Church. "Get the *Trentonian* for 10 cents" read the ad slapped to the side of the box.

It was then and there that I learned to be careful who you share your ideas with, because chances are they will take them and use them to their advantage, not yours. Lesson learned: life and business dealings are not always fair.

In retaliation, the following week I stopped ordering the extra papers from my new district manager. Instead, I rearranged my route so that I would go to the paper box first. I would deposit my dime, then take the entire bundle of papers from the box, leaving it empty so that even if someone put their dime in, they would not receive a paper.

I then proceeded to perform my morning run as normal. Only now, I delivered the twelve extra papers the manager had directed me to as well as the twelve I would normally do, but I had not paid for them.

Once I made my run, I would end up at the bus stop out front of the church and sell all that I could as usual out of my basket on my bike. In most cases for a quarter and a "Keep the change, buddy!"

When the bus would leave, I deposited another dime in the slot and returned whatever papers I had left—there were never very many—back in the company's paper box.

I remember turning from the box one morning and looking at the church marquee, the place where the preacher would put his verse for the week: "Know ye not that they who run in a race run all, but one receiveth the prize? So run, that ye may obtain" (1 Corinthians 9:24).

I knew I would surely have to listen extra hard that Sunday when he spoke, because to my way of thinking, God had just told me to run my business to win, not just to exist.

Eventually, I took over the other two *Trentonian* paper routes in town, when the boys who did them moved on. By the time I gave up my three routes at the beginning of sophomore year, I was delivering or selling over three hundred newspapers daily. I remember that the guy who took over the routes, when I gave them up, used his car to make the deliveries ... there would never be any more paperboys in Hopewell.

In 2014, there was an attack on a large electric substation in California that panicked the electric utility industry and, more importantly, the government in Washington, DC. Theories ranged from disgruntled employees to domestic terrorists attacking the station. Through a series of timely events, a potential catastrophe was thwarted. However, the potential devastation was theorized by the government and others in my business sphere, which resulted in Congress enacting what became known as the Critical Infrastructure Protection Act of 2014 (CIP-14). It isn't necessary to delve into the details of the incident or the terms of the act. However, this grabbed the attention of three multinational companies and their respective subsidiaries in the fence business, and they focused on the utility industry, specifically on substation fencing.

Their thought process ran amuck at the time, but suffice it to say their so-called internal experts determined that because CIP-14 was literally an act of Congress, there would be funding to upgrade and replace *every* substation fence in America. All in the name of protecting us from home-grown terrorism. To compound this misinformed premise, they did the math wrong. Their misguided belief, in my opinion, was that somehow funding would soon become available for hundreds of thousands of substations to be upgraded with new security fencing.

I could see in my mind's eye the exaggerated conversations taking place in conference rooms across the three multinational fence companies when considering the effects of CIP-14 on the electric utility industry.

I don't believe I need to run this fictitious calculation out for you, but by the time the projections reached the home offices in Sweden, Japan, and South Africa, the numbers must have been staggering. Talk about having goals that make others uncomfortable! This was that on steroids. The problem, in my opinion, was that CIP-14 was an unfunded mandate, little more than a suggestion by the current administration, put out for public consumption with no teeth. Unless, of course, your portion of the electric grid serviced the District of

Columbia and the political corridors of the US government. Then, miraculously, there was funding. But I digress.

An industry where VANQUISH had very little competition previously now had three major players fighting for scraps to somehow salvage their astronomic sales projections for security fence projects that never materialized. At least not in the volumes they had projected to upper management. And so these three multinational companies eventually sent their representatives into my tiny conference room in Kannapolis, North Carolina, to convince this simple "country bumpkin" into spilling the secrets to the success of VANQUISH.

After years of building the VANQUISH brand and the VANQUISH business, my largest customer asked me to partner my company with these larger international fence manufacturing companies. In an effort to comply, I reluctantly agreed to work with one directly and two partially. I agreed to allow my patented Animal Mitigation System to be installed on their security fence solutions. Everything in my gut told me not to do this—but I did it just the same. Just like working with that new district manager as a kid, I shared with them how and why my system worked. Even though we had signed all the nondisclosure agreements and marked all the drawings confidential, these three companies went on to market, each in their own way, *my* product as if they had invented it and owned the rights to it. Claiming that although I had been manufacturing, building, selling, and installing my *patented system* for over seventeen years now, we somehow had developed this together. The outcome of this infringement is still under investigation and is in the hands of legal counsel at the time of this writing.

The point I want to drive home is twofold: (1) when someone is bent on stealing from you, there is a good chance you can't stop them, and (2) you should continually do everything you can to protect your ideas and your investment in those ideas, even if you suffer a loss in the end.

In my forced dealings with these three companies, I did not share all, but I did share too much, and each company in turn has copied something VANQUISH had perfected and claimed it for their own. Lesson learned: Share with no one perceived to be a competitor, no matter how much they think you will grow the business together if you share your thoughts. And more important, know that patents are only as good as your pockets are deep enough to defend them. In my case, neither had a good outcome.

However, I did not let these incidents stop me. Following Mark Twain's words of guidance, with courage, I continue even today to take risks, having the strength to be compassionate, and the wisdom to be humble. Remembering that courage is the foundation of integrity, I continue to change the game by creating new dreams, new products, and new goals that make the competition uncomfortable.

I originally agreed to work with these other companies out of my desire to grow VANQUISH. I reasoned that if these three companies would have played fair, I would be installing my system on their fences. And since my product was patented, it would be a no-brainer for them to give me my fair share. I could not have been naiver about the ways of the world and big business.

In order for VANQUISH to grow and to have the chance of someday becoming great, I knew that I needed a good product, a good offering, a good brand, and good branding, *and* I needed a proficient team of people. I could not do it all on my own. I needed talents, skills, and experiences I did not presently possess. I needed individuals, a cadre of folks that I could invite to play in my sandbox. To line up beside me and forge the path that, in my eyes, VANQUISH was destined to travel in the quest to fulfill my desire for *great*. I needed to surround myself with people that would push me to do better. I did not want drama or negativity. I wanted an environment where I could foster a group whose primary objective was for higher goals and higher motivation toward *great*. I wanted good times and positive energy. No jealousy or hatred. Simply a team that would bring out the absolute best in each other. And I was all in when I read *Good to Great*, especially when Collins said, "The vast majority of companies never become great, precisely because the vast majority become quite good—and that is their main problem."[10]

My dreams were so big that they made those around me uncomfortable. My vision and goals for VANQUISH were and still are big to this day. I spent the first fifteen years in business having everyone in the industry wondering what VANQUISH was doing that was so different. My accomplishments in the market were perceived as so great that the three multinational companies that one might consider my competition were left wondering how and why VANQUISH was able to accomplish what we were doing. And how we became such a force in the industry. What they did not realize is that I was the original thought leader in the industry. I set out by *listening* to my customers and *hearing* their pain points, then offering an *exact* solution to their problem. I did not push them into my one-size-fits-all solution. In a relatively short period of time, fifteen years to be exact, I changed the narrative, the market expectation, and set the standard by which all others would be judged.

This did not happen by accident. This happened because I built a team of individuals who each brought a different set of expertise

---

10 Jim Collins, *Good to Great* (New York: Harper Business, 2001), 1.

and experiences to the table. More important, we practiced the most essential quality of leadership: intellectual honesty.

Jack Welch once said that the most important quality of leadership is the "reality principle." He defined this as the ability to see the world as it really is, not as you wish it were. He would begin every meeting to discuss a goal or a problem with the question "What's the reality?"

> **We practiced the most essential quality of leadership: intellectual honesty.**

It was Peter Drucker who referred to this quality as "intellectual honesty," meaning dealing with the facts exactly as they are before attempting to solve a problem or make a decision. I personalized this for my team into the ability to be completely honest and objective with ourselves when faced with a decision at VANQUISH. We needed to be—and continue to be—completely honest with where we are today, where we want to be tomorrow, and how we plan to get there given the resources available to us at any moment.

Another principle that has guided my team is best summed up in another quote by Jack Welch: "If the rate of change on the outside exceeds the rate of change on the inside, the end is near." I never want the end of VANQUISH to be near, at least not while I still have an ounce of life in me.

I have said it before, but it deserves repeating here: I believe that as an entrepreneur I need to "be there before I get there." Said another way: "act like you've been here before." In business, I must be confident in my own abilities, even when I know I am lacking. People want to be around and associated with successful people. No one wakes up in the morning and intentionally says, "I think I will hang out with a bunch of losers today."

The people I want to work with in business certainly do not want to listen to or interact with individuals who do not appear to be confident in their solutions. As the face and voice of my company, my brand, I need to be confident in what I know and what I am selling. I need to invest in myself by doing my homework in advance. I need to know the subject. Know the problem. Know the solution. Make the sale. Simple to say, but much harder to do.

"Whether you think you can, or you think you can't, you are right." Henry Ford is credited with having said those words. I believe most people are not stopped by outside forces; they are stopped by their own internal limitations. They succumb to their internal fears much too easily. Starting a business of any kind and of any size takes large amounts of courage. Yes, risk is involved! It has been said that a real entrepreneur is one who flies without a safety net. I can tell you firsthand from my own experiences that is true. Especially since I started my venture underfunded, which always seemed contradictory to me by the sheer definition of the word *entrepreneur* according to *Webster's Dictionary*: one who takes on greater-than-normal financial risks in order to organize and operate a business or businesses. From my experiences and to my way of thinking, if I'd had all the necessary funding I'd needed, I would most likely have done something different with my money. Like take less risk.

In his book *The Power of Positive Thinking*, Norman Vincent Peale states, "Life cannot deny itself to the person who gives life his or her all. But most people, unfortunately, don't do that. In fact, very few people do, and this is a tragic cause of failure, or, if not failure, it is the reason we only half attain."[11]

When I looked around, I found so many people in my universe that this simple statement applied to—people who were just doing the bare minimum to get by. Working nine to five in dead-end jobs that they hated, doing absolutely nothing to make life better for themselves or those around them. Or worse, living a life that had no excitement, no purpose; living in relationships that they appeared to be only half invested in.

I know it is not completely true, but I noticed that those I called "morning people" tended to greet life as if it was a gift, and by comparison, those who were not morning people dreaded the start of each day, which to my way of thinking did not embrace the day as if it were a gift. Being an eternal optimist myself, I soon came to realize that if I was to live a life worth remembering, I needed to be the cause. I needed to learn to expect good things from life, and by the laws of nature, I needed to grow to expect every day to be a wonder, not a chore. Yes, days could be bad, but if I did not start the day on a high note, then it would surely be a drag on my emotions and my expectations.

Even in my youth, I realized I needed to do my part. I needed to get up each day and embrace the new opportunity I was given with the start of each day. I needed to walk by faith, not by sight. I needed to work hard to be the cause of every new opportunity that I firmly believed would eventually come my way.

During my years of employment at Prudential Securities as an investment advisor, I worked with a guy who would cold-call prospective investors with the opening line of knocking on his desk into the phone receiver and saying "Do you hear that? That is opportu-

11   Norman Vincent Peale, *The Power of Positive Thinking*, 110.

nity knocking, Mrs. Jones!" For me, every sunrise was opportunity knocking.

In *Good to Great*, Collins writes[12]

good is the enemy of great, and that is one of the key reasons why we have so little that becomes great. We don't have great schools, principally because we have good schools. We don't have great government principally because we have good government. Few people attain great lives, in large part because it is just so easy to settle for a good life. The vast majority of companies never become great, precisely because the vast majority become quite good—and that is their main problem.

I developed an attitude of wanting to be great. I wanted to be a great husband, a great father, a great friend, a great employee, a great boss, a great business leader. Most of all I wanted to build something great! Something to live on long past my time. To leave the little postage stamp of the world that was to be marked as my life better than I found it. I wanted to give life my all! I did not want to half attain.

Although it took me twenty years to realize and to clearly see the two roads diverging in the woods and taking the one that would lead me to create a business called VANQUISH, I've lived each day before and after as if I were the cause of my own destiny. I began to sow seeds that I knew I might someday harvest, and in so doing, reap bountifully. I gave everything I did my all. I made a commitment to my wife. I made a commitment to my children. I made a commitment to every job I ever had to be the best and to bring more to the

---

12   Collins, *Good to Great*, 1.

table than I took. I studied. I learned. I strived to develop myself to be a better person.

Yes, I became demanding both of myself and others. I would not say I became a perfectionist or a tyrant, but I worked *toward* perfection with the understanding that if I failed while trying to be great, I knew there was a hope that I would land close to great. Which, again, to my way of thinking, was one step closer to my goal of being great. If I failed while attempting, I held the belief that in landing in a place better than where I had been meant I was still a step closer toward my goal of being great. I never accepted just doing enough, half attaining, as being okay for myself.

In the early years of VANQUISH—the years before I had employees and the years that I had employees—people in my life would watch me work tirelessly all day, every day. They would see me work long hours and on weekends and travel what seemed like all the time, taking meeting after meeting. Visiting jobsites and potential jobsites. Visiting customers and potential customers all over the country. They would marvel and wonder what drove me. The answer was simple: I personally strived every day for greatness. I was, and still am to this day, not willing to accept good over great. I believe, as does Jim Collins, that good is truly the enemy of great. Although I don't see good as failure, not striving for great is a flaw I do not want in my life. I would jokingly tell people close to me that VANQUISH was my mistress, and when she called, I came running. If I was going to be away from my wife and my family, it better be worth it. VANQUISH was to be great, or there was no sense in me investing in it. The company took all that I had and, in return, has afforded me all that I've wanted, including giving my wife, my family, and myself all that I felt we deserved. As a result of my efforts and investment, VANQUISH gave me personal satisfaction in knowing I was working toward the achievement of great and ultimately a personal sense of accomplishment.

As I sit in my chair on the island cliff that I have become so fond of, cigar in hand, contemplating life and reflecting on the future, I look out over the rolling blue waters and realize that, just like the waves endlessly breaking onto the shore, the pursuit of great is never ending. In moments like this, I take comfort in knowing that not accepting good and striving for great is what makes the journey even more satisfying. Or, put another way, when putting myself as a four out of five on my employee evaluation sheet leaves me room for improvement, the goal of obtaining a five is always a step toward making myself and my business great.

VANQUISH has always been flexible enough and strong enough to be the industry thought leader in this space since its inception. By being in tune with our industry and listening rather than telling, we expanded our offering to incorporate new fence systems for the market. We went from being the original twenty-year-tested animal mitigation company to changing our focus to become the leader in the community acceptance of utilities substation. This

We are the best value for the dollar, and we go where that thought process is appreciated.

simple change in our offerings and directions of product advancement is what allowed us to turn the tables on the three multinational companies that came knocking on our door. While they chase after the CIP security fence projects, we drove off in an entirely new direction to, once again, become the thought leader for substation neighborhood acceptance.

In so doing, we continued the practice inspired by Jack Welch when he said if you don't have a competitive advantage, don't compete. VANQUISH does not strive to be the low-cost provider in anything we do. We are the best value for the dollar, and we go where that thought process is appreciated.

My sales team and I were attending an IEEE trade show in Chicago one year when a representative of what I call an alternative solutions provider showed his face in my booth. He looked down at my countertop and pointed to a stress ball–type squirrel my assistant had made as a giveaway for the show. It had the name VANQUISH across its belly. People loved them, and we had been giving them out at trade shows for a few years by this point. To my understanding, this individual had recently taken a management position at an alternative solutions provider. Since his company did not offer a perimeter fence solution to animal mitigation, I did not think he was a direct competitor, but he thought otherwise.

A little backstory.

This particular company, Company X, had gone through bankruptcy and been sold a number of times over the last twenty years. Its original inception was approximately ten years before VANQUISH came into existence. Company X offered one of the alternative solutions I had studied prior to starting my business. One of my mainstay customers at that time had previously used an alternative solution from Company X. However, a ten-year study conducted by my customer found that Company X's system was only 80 percent effective; one in five had failed in the field. It was obvious the individual standing in my booth, waving his arms in anger, knew very little about the history of the animal mitigation industry.

As he grew more aggressive toward me for "copying" his success, I responded, "I've heard you, and this is not the place for this type of conversation." Then I asked him to leave. He then grabbed a stress squirrel off the counter and said, "You copied my idea."

When I told him he was crazy, he threw the squirrel at me but missed. I looked at him and said, "Now what? Do we get in a brawl here like on the grade school playground?"

He proceeded to yell more obscenities at my sales team and me as he slowly backed away from my booth. I remember his last words as he turned and walked away: "You never had an original idea in your life!" Which was extremely ironic, because everything that I had accomplished—and continue to accomplish—through VANQUISH is in every way original and different from my competition.

My team and I had a good laugh, and for a few years after that incident our rally cry became "You never had an original idea in your life!" Especially after the three multinational companies sent their teams in to copy my ideas right down to the last detail in our drawings. This action on their part could have killed my company and stopped me cold. But as I've learned throughout my life, obstacles are never insurmountable; they simply present new opportunities to grow my business.

I "never had an original idea" in my life? Ha! Thank you very much.

CHAPTER SEVEN
CHANNEL MARKERS

If I share with a competitor, I lose. Share with no one perceived to be a competitor.

This rule was learned the hard way. It is safer to assume that every perceived competitor or alternative solutions provider is out to steal my intellectual property. Therefore, I should strive to protect it at all costs.

Intellectual property rights and patents are only as good as my pockets are deep enough to defend them in court.

The old adage from my youth "My father is bigger than your father" is the best way I know to explain this. The bigger the law firm the competition has, the harder it is to stop them from stealing from me. The money I spend to obtain patents and to defend patents needs to be considered before investing in future patents for my ideas.

My strategy for competing in the market space I choose must involve a different set of activities designed to deliver superior value to my customers if I am to grow my business.

I must make the way I think about the value proposition I put into the universe different from my competitors, if I am to offer a superior value for my customer's investment dollars. This rule was inspired by Mike Porter, author of *Competitive Strategy*, and introduced to me by the authors of *Playing to Win*.

Dream so big that I make those around me uncomfortable.

This rule is based on the popular BHAG principle: do the impossible by setting Big Hairy Audacious Goals for yourself and your team. The example often cited is the goal of being the first to land on the moon in the early 1960s.

My business needs to adapt to changing markets, or it will cease to exist.

This rule was also inspired by Jack Welch. His rule read: "If the rate of change on the outside exceeds the rate of change on the inside, the end is near."

The answer will always be no if I don't ask for what I want.

Pretty simple rule, but I am amazed at how many times in my life I did not ask, and therefore I did not receive. In life, in business, and specifically in sales, if I don't ask for the order, I will surely never get it. So I developed a habit of asking for the order every time. I did not always get it, but I believe I am a success today because I got a yes more times than I got a no—which was certain if I did not ask.

If I don't have a competitive advantage, I don't compete.

This rule was also inspired by Jack Welch. If I cannot be number one or number two in my space, I should not compete. When the three multinational fence manufacturers invaded my market space for a specific security solution, I moved my company's focus away from the shining object of their desire. This process allowed me to keep the lion's share of the customers' business in my space while conceding the smaller market to the competition, which ultimately eliminated their ability to compete with me.

CHAPTER EIGHT

The Worst Thing Someone Can Say Is No

If you have an important point to make, don't try to be subtle or clever. Use a pile driver. Hit the point once. Then come back and hit it again. Then hit it a third time with a tremendous whack.

—*WINSTON S. CHURCHILL*

By the end of 2014, VANQUISH had grown to thirty-five employees with over $4 million in equipment and $2.5 million invested in sellable inventory, and it had just topped $10 million in gross sales. VANQUISH had thoroughly outgrown the facility I'd bought in 2013, and I was once again looking for more room to grow. A far cry from the lows of 2008 through 2010, when a weaker version of me might have called it quits, accepted the mantle of failure, and, at the age of fifty-two, slithered back to rewrite my résumé in preparation for a new job search and a trip down the road most traveled.

When I started my quest in 2001, in all honesty I had no idea the scope of the business I would be building when I made my first phone calls to the electric utilities to discover if there really was a need for keeping small crawling animals out of substations. I had larger-than-life dreams and lofty aspirations of building something new and big by my standards, yes. But to the scale that VANQUISH had become in the industry, no.

I also had no idea at the time that fourteen years later, a man named Peter Thiel would write a book in which he would confirm many of my core beliefs. Thiel describes that when you make something, "it's easier to copy a model than to make something new. Doing what we already know how to do takes the world from *1 to n*,[13] adding more of something familiar. But every time we create something new, we go from *0 to 1*. The act of creation is singular, as is the moment of creation, and the result is something fresh and strange."[14]

By what seemed to me to be sheer common sense, according to Thiel I was actually uniquely following the process of creating something new. I was effectively taking business from literally zero to one.

I quote Thiel once again: "Doing something different is what's truly good for society—and it's also what allows a business to profit by monopolizing a new market. The best projects are likely to be overlooked, not trumpeted by a crowd: the best problems to work on are often the ones nobody else even tries to solve."[15]

---

13 Just so you, the reader, will understand, I interpreted *n* to mean something not new or nil, zero, the same level.

14 Peter Thiel, *Zero to One*, preface.

15 Thiel, *Zero to One*, 166.

In reading his book, I began to see what I had done reflected in his writings and, more importantly, the value in what I had done. I had effectively created something new in that I was transforming an existing asset on the customer's accounting books into a viable solution to a real problem. I was doing it in a way that no one else had done up to this point in time. I was not only saving my customers money by eliminating costly repairs and replacement of high-dollar substation apparatuses damaged by animals through their interaction with the equipment. I was increasing their reliability statistics in the eyes of the regulators. All by reducing animal-caused power outages at the substation level. By their words, their ROI was worth the investment in VANQUISH Systems every time.

> **As a result of my initial actions, I had a monopoly on my market space for over twenty years.**

Furthermore, as a result of my initial actions, I had a monopoly on my market space for over twenty years. Simply by focusing on a fragment of the industry and a specific problem in that segment that no one else seemed interested in addressing. True to Thiel's deduction, I did it with no great fanfare—untrumpeted!

Thiel goes on to say that "unless they invest in the difficult task of creating new things, American companies will fail in the future no matter how big their profits remain today."[16] Armed with this additional piece of advice from 2014 and the added 2017 interest the three multinational steel fence companies had just shown in the space VANQUISH currently occupies as a result of CIP-14. We instinctively moved the cheese, as they say!

---

16   Thiel, *Zero to One*, 166.

VANQUISH has pushed forward into new markets with new products. Products the steel fence manufacturers cannot easily replicate. This move does open us up to additional competitors. Or, as I like to say, alternative solution providers. VANQUISH is going about this addition to our offerings in the same way as we did with animal mitigation all those years ago. We are taking the world from zero to one once again by offering nonconductive, decorative perimeter systems, at a fraction of the install costs associated with concrete structures. All with the satisfaction of addressing the community-acceptance piece of the puzzle for our customers. Effectively we have found another market not trumpeted yet.

—————————————

Through the experiences in my years of business, I found that, in life and especially in owning my own business, no matter the outcome, I had to put my all into the process. And so for almost twenty years, I have been the thought leader in the industry, simply by "owning it" from day one. I was one of the unfortunate ones who got to taste Wall Street and then suffer through the demise of the dot-com era. I was obviously a little late to the party in my career at JAGFN. But according to Thiel, I was one of the lucky ones who rode the wave of the economy that went from "bricks to clicks and back to bricks again." Lucky for me, I learned the hard way that if I like something or go after something because everyone else is doing it, I'm most likely going in the wrong direction.

As a result, I learned that in business you need to be original in your thinking. You need to come up with that product or service that makes your company unique. I further believed, instinctively, that as an entrepreneur I needed to be in an industry under the radar. By addressing my fatal flaw all those years ago, I had done what Thiel would suggest years later: if my product needed advertising, it was not good enough for the market.

Thiel states that customers don't care about any particular technology unless it solves a particular problem in a superior way. In VANQUISH, I offered a large industry a solution to a problem that helped keep the lights on. I was not offering to make electricity or make it cheaper, and in that regard, it was not the big play that the generation or distribution of electricity was; but it was a strong contribution to relieving financial pain for my present and future customers. I was operating under the radar in such a way that no multinational company had me in their sights until I was financially strong enough to hold my own, thus mitigating my fatal flaw at the start of my business.

When I started in 2001, I had created a way to keep small crawling animals out of electric utility substations, and I was solving a problem that up until then had not been addressed sufficiently. By 2014, I learned that I, in fact, was taking the world and my company from *zero to one*! By 2017, if I had any doubts about the points I just outlined, they were dissipated when the three major players in the fence industry copied my patented system and sold it as if they had invented it themselves.

Instinctively I learned through my years of working for others a few more concepts and lessons that have served me well. There's another point I feel worth mentioning, which came to me while I worked at Prudential Securities, where I was required to call complete strangers in order to make the business of being a stockbroker work.

When starting out with any new venture, the first phone call, the first presentation, that I had to make to engage a complete stranger was one of the hardest. People say that the phone weighs a hundred pounds that day, and they are right. I had to summon all that I had in me to pick it up and make the call. I wish I could tell you there is some secret to how to make that less painful, but I cannot. The only thing I can tell you is I had to make the call!

My future depended on it. It is my experience that in that moment I have got to have the mindset "I have been here before." And so I practiced that call, my words, my questions, my answers, daily. Until I had the confidence to make the call as if I had done it a thousand times already. Which then became reality, because I did have to make the call and many more like it, to survive and thrive.

It has been said that Martin Luther King Jr., one of the greatest speakers of all time, would write his speeches out longhand and then memorize them. He practiced reciting them until he knew every word, every inflection, every pause, by heart. Then he would turn the paper over on the podium and recite the entire speech from memory. To my way of thinking, I needed to imitate that process if I was to come across as authentic to the people when speaking passionately about what I and VANQUISH could do for them.

I am also a firm believer in visualization; it's something I've done ever since I read *The Power of Positive Thinking*. I always want to be confident in what I know and what I am doing. I would visualize in my mind's eye what success looked like for me. I saw myself making the presentation; I saw myself answering the hard questions; I saw myself closing the deal. In

> **I saw myself in my mind's eye building my business one step at a time.**

truth I saw myself in my mind's eye building my business one step at a time. Effectively, I was there before I got there. I practice this process every day. I also tell my staff before every presentation "Close your eyes and visualize in your mind's eye what success looks like for you."

I practice this mindset in every aspect of my life and business. I saw the finished product and service in my mind, even though some of the details would change in real life. I saw the people in the room asking questions and visualized how I would answer them long before I got to that day. Above all, I saw myself making the sale. And by *sale*, I don't mean having someone sign on the dotted line and giving me a check, although that would be the end goal. Making the sale is me convincing the customer to hear me out. That means my thought process needs to be clear in my mind first and foremost; otherwise, I'll never convince anyone of anything. After all, the sale is everything.

I cannot emphasize enough how important it is to see yourself in the moment long before you get there. Most of what goes on in our minds daily might scare others. For me, knowing how my mind works would most likely give people pause. I find it is natural to be nervous, especially if you have never actually created something from nothing. Especially if you have never started or built a business, come up with a service, or made the sale of your own product before.

Being passionate helps, but being confident, in my opinion, is the most important tool needed to do what you see in your mind's eye—especially closing the sale. The potential customer must believe you believe in your business and what you are doing and that you will deliver on your promise before they ever consider purchasing from you.

Telling people "This is my first time" only serves to weaken your argument. You must believe in yourself and what you are doing, and you have to exude that belief in your entire interaction with the client. You have got to come across as if you have been in this exact moment before and won the business.

By now you will realize that right up there with *Good to Great*, Thiel's book *Zero to One* has had tremendous influence on my way of thinking. It is not so much that both books taught me new information; rather they confirmed my intuition and put into words the wisdom I've used as channel markers in formulating how I viewed the world and my business and its ultimate position in the river of life.

As a result, I have formulated that many people believe in what I have come to call the "Field of Dreams" system when starting a business: If you build it, they will come. Unfortunately, in my experience, this is rarely the case. Especially when building a start-up business. I find you have to first go out and get customers; then potential customers will come to you. Some will say that you have to be a good salesperson with a good gift of gab. I prefer to identify it as having what the customer needs when they need it, and that comes through listening, not talking. Learning when to present a solution to the customer's pain only after identifying their pain.

The truth is that most people, by nature, say "No, I am not interested" before you even get in the door. If you want a potential customer to take you seriously, you need a really good knock. This is an opening that shows you care, you listen, and you understand the problem from *their* point of view, all before you present a solution, your solution.

In my case, I could not say I supplied fences, because fences are a dime a dozen, and I would end up talking to facilities managers who buy fences from the lowest bidder. My knock came in the form of a call to the folks in charge of keeping the power *on*. And my pitch was "How much does a power outage cost you?" and "What is it worth to you to increase your reliability at the substation level?"

What I can also tell you from making all those calls, in the beginning and all the years since, is it became clear that animal mitigation was a big deal for electric utilities. It also became very clear there is a difference between the selling of a fence that deters small crawling animals and the sale of a system that actually increases reliability. Meaning when it came to keeping the power on to customers, the utility would earn more revenue; literally, when the power is out the meter stops running, and so does the electric bill we all pay. After all, we will not pay for what we don't get. The bottom line is that, as I have mentioned before, I learned a valuable lesson: among other things, if I was to have success, I would need to sell value in prevention versus selling a physical fence as a material substance.

Drawing my conclusion from this activity is that the worst thing someone can say is no!

No, I don't want to talk to you. No, I am not interested. No, thank you. No, you cannot have my business. Which reminds me of my days at Prudential, when I would think, "Okay, thank you; now I am one more *no* closer to a *yes*." I learned to keep my focus on getting *no* out of the way so I can hear the wonderful sound of the word *yes!*

CHAPTER EIGHT
CHANNEL MARKERS

Whatever I do in business and in life, I need to lean into it.

The outcome, good or bad, doesn't matter as much as the fact that I have put my all into it, whatever *it* is. The only chance I have to succeed is by showing up and being there in that moment.

I need a really good knock if I am ever going to get people to listen to me.

Most doors in the world are closed to me, so when I find one that I want to go through, I better be damn sure I have an interesting knock.

If I like something because I think other people are going to like it, it's a sure bet no one will like it.

Pretty self-explanatory, but just the same, I need to be original in my thinking and do something because it adds value to me *and* to those I am willing to share my thoughts and actions with.

Everything I think is important isn't. Everything I think is unimportant turns out to be important.

Again, pretty self-explanatory. Unfortunately, my experiences have proven this has happened to me more often than I care to admit. Underscoring my need to think hard and long about the actions I am about to take.

Author's note: although I had developed an earlier version of these channel markers, they were refined after seeing a similar version recited in the movie distributed by DreamWorks and Disney Studios in 2012 titled *People Like Us.*

CHAPTER NINE

Don't Start with the Focus on Sales

Competition is overrated. In practice it is quite destructive and should be avoided wherever possible. Much better than fighting for scraps in existing markets is to create and own new ones.

—PETER THIEL

My original ideas for how to market the solutions offered by VANQUISH have evolved over the years. I was fortunate in that my original system worked exceptionally well. Over twenty years now, and it is still 100 percent effective at keeping small crawling animals out of substations. Which, simply stated, means every station that had a history of animal-caused outages. Once a VANQUISH system was installed, the outages caused by animals ceased to happen.

The unintentional, albeit welcomed, consequence was that with the elimination of animal-caused outages, electric utilities reliability numbers increased, and thus customer satisfaction was raised. No one wants to look at a substation in their neighborhood, but worse is looking at a substation and your power being out at the same time. That is unsatisfactory no matter how you slice it.

I have said many times, what we do is not rocket science. That statement does not make it any less important; to my way of thinking, I stumbled on a larger problem solved simply by taking care of the smaller problem. Thus, making what we do invaluable to the industry and specifically our customers. And more importantly to their customers.

In my search for a problem to solve, and to give my business meaning, I focused on the problem of keeping animals out. However, I was not fully engaged with the bigger-picture problem. Instead, I was small-sighted on a detail I could address, which, quite by accident, introduced me to what I found to be the greater value of my proposition. Over the years, as my VANQUISH team grew, we have learned to look at the big picture effect of what we do more carefully in order to stay relevant in current times.

If I could supply a viable solution, I would be entitled to a piece of the market.

So how did we get there?

In 2001, it was my intention to start a business of my own. I looked to solve a known issue in an industry that was already spending money trying to find a solution to the problem I was going to address. My initial thought process was there were no clear or real effective solutions currently available. There were plenty of alternatives but no clear-cut solve. Which meant that if I could supply a viable solution, I would be entitled to a piece of the market. This small commonsense approach, I believe, will work for anyone wanting to start a business. The utility market is not unique in this matter; it just happens to be where I decided to play.

Let me explain.

In 2013, A. G. Lafley, former CEO of Procter & Gamble, along with Roger Martin, dean of Toronto's Rotman School of Management, wrote a book called *Playing to Win: How Strategy Really Works*. In their book, they confirmed for me what I had instinctively, and by accident, discovered when I formed my business. They described the five choices that needed to be at the heart of any winning business strategy: a winning aspiration, where to play, how to win, core capabilities, and management systems. They called it *The Playbook: Five Choices, One Framework, One Process*. I highly recommend that this book be on your must-read list if you are considering starting a business. It is required reading for VANQUISH management hires ever since I found it a few years back. We live by the notes outlined in its pages.

Having a strategy outlined by the *Playing to Win* platform sounds easy, but according to Lafley, most companies, large and small, don't do it effectively. Again, I refer to my commonsense good fortune of having developed my own strategy. And then having it reaffirmed by this book makes it worth sharing with you here. I'll lay it out at the thirty-thousand-foot level for understanding. The details are much more engrained and granule, too much for this writing.

My aspirations. I originally looked at and listened to what my potential customers were faced with, the problem, their problem. Then I developed a product to address their needs, their desires, their wants. My aspirations were to create a safe and secure environment, intimidating to intruders while adding to the overall appearance and protection of assets. My mission and vision were not to just sell more fences.

Where to play. I then defined where I would play, even though I did not define it as such back then. I defined the market space I would operate in. Meaning I would not try to be everything to everyone in every industry that used a perimeter fence. My goal was to stay specifically in the electric-substation arena. Targeting the prevention of animals gaining access to a controlled area. Do one thing, and do it the best I possibly could, before I would ever consider doing a second thing.

How to win. What did winning look like? I decided almost from the start that I needed to win, and I defined how I would win. I would supply a 100 percent effective solution from day one. No excuses. Which does not sound odd at first. But if you realize that in the space I was operating, 50–80 percent effectiveness rates were considered acceptable by my future customers. I had people from the largest electric utilities in the country tell me that if I could eliminate one or two animal-caused outages a year, I would be considered a success. No one expected 100 percent success. A concept that made no sense to me. How do you buy something knowing there is a 20–50 percent chance it will fail?

I defined how I would win: quality materials manufactured, assembled, and installed in the most cost effective and efficient way possible. Offer a great product at a fair price. I was clear on my core capabilities from the start. Do one thing right, and do it every time the same way. My promise: others claim their product is good, but ours does what you think it should.

Management systems. In the beginning, when I was the only employee, by default management systems were in place to ensure the plan would be funded and managed. There would be no obstacles to prevent this plan from working, and I was not going to roadblock myself on this. Today, there are systems in place to protect the strategic plan of VANQUISH.

I don't want to mislead you by oversimplifying the issues. This chapter, by design, outlines my good fortune in that the space I chose to operate, where I chose to play, was the ideal spot for all the reasons I outlined previously. Having this strong field advantage, I was afforded the opportunity to stay focused on the business at hand and my offerings to my customers.

I had determined my solutions would be second to none in quality of materials, quality of design, and quality of effectiveness. Having found an industry that was willing to accept so much less from the alternative solutions made my offerings so much more attractive to them. Then factor in that my standards for myself, my products, my system, and VANQUISH were so high I could not help but impress, as they say. However, I did not completely realize the good fortune I started with, so I attacked the market as if I was the loser trying to gain field advantage. The combination of high standards and attacking the market not only launched me to the head of the pack but also catapulted me out front. Couple this good fortune and hard work with the fact that I had chosen to focus on a space with minimal competition; there was no limit to my success in the early years. By the time I realized all this, I was then fully prepared to capitalize on it. Building a base that after twenty years in service still leaves me in the winning position. It has also afforded me opportunities most start-up businesses might not be able to boast about.

I defined my core values as a company from day one:

- Ingenuity—Design safe, long-lasting solutions.

- Integrity—Real in all we do, by offering superior solutions at reasonable margins.

- Passion—Unrivaled vision, innovation, and execution.

- Quality—We're here to help, from concept to installation.

I reasoned that if I wanted to make my product and service everything it could be, they need to be repeatedly reexamined for ways to be improved with the full understanding that there will be modifications. Sometimes extensive modifications, based on how my customers react to what I have supplied. I made it my mission for VANQUISH and my systems to be under a constant state of review; to find our shortcomings and areas in need of improvement, which to my way of thinking is the entire try-fail-improve-and-repeat-process we must continually go through as a company. To that end, for more than twenty years, VANQUISH, the original animal mitigation specialist, has offered exceptional quality and supreme value. We pride ourselves on being an innovator in the field and look forward to continuing work with electric utilities to solve problems in the future.

> **The quality of what I sell should be second to none and should be my primary goal as a company.**

I decided long ago that I must challenge myself to embrace fear and failure not only so they don't defeat me but, more importantly, so that I am giving my customers the best I have to offer on any given day. The quality of what I sell should be second to none and should be my primary goal as a company. I never want to sell an inferior product just to gain market share. I always sell a quality product at a quality price. I focus my efforts to maintain the best possible product and service I can give. I made it a rule long ago that VANQUISH will never be thought of as the low-cost provider. Which is the whole reason I offer a twenty-five-year warranty on my solutions.

I titled this chapter "Don't Start with the Focus on Sales" because I never did. Yes, I need sales to survive and thrive, but that was never my focus. I believed, as Peter Thiel so clearly stated, that if you make your product worth the price, then customers will find you. I believed I needed to start by making what I offer worth the purchase price to the customer; then the sales would come.

I always want my product and service to be considered second to none. This strategy allows me to deliver a quality return on investment for my client, which, to my way of thinking, will also drive sales. I never want to be so focused on making the sale that I diminish the VANQUISH brand.

One last thought. Years ago, for one of my birthdays, I had the opportunity to visit the Jack Daniel's Distillery in Lynchburg, Tennessee. While on the tour, we made our way through what was once Mr. Daniel's office, and on the wall was this simple sign with the words "Every Day We Make It, We'll Make It the Best We Can." I loved it! So clean, so simple, so perfect. So I adapted my own version. At VANQUISH, we say, "Every Day We Make It, We Will Make It the Best We Can." I hope Mr. Daniel doesn't mind. I think the rule needs no explanation.

CHAPTER NINE
CHANNEL MARKERS

The quality of what I sell should be second to none and should be my primary goal.

I never want to sell an inferior product just to gain market share. I always sell a quality product at a quality price. I focus my efforts to maintain the best possible product and service I can give.

Make what I offer worth the purchase price to the customer, and sales will come.

I want my product and service to always be considered second to none. This strategy allows me to deliver a quality return on investment for my client, which, to my way of thinking, will drive sales. I never want to be so focused on making the sale that I diminish the VANQUISH brand.

"Every Day We Make It, We Will Make It the Best We Can."

I adopted this rule after visiting the Jack Daniel's Distillery in Lynchburg, Tennessee, and saw Jack's version hanging in what had been his office. I think the rule needs no explanation.

CHAPTER TEN

The More the Storm, the More the Strength

> The brave man is not he who does not feel
> afraid, but he who conquers that fear.
>
> *—NELSON MANDELA*

We've all heard the saying "It is always the darkest just before the dawn." I can tell you from experience that many times it gets dark when building your business. My life and my firsthand experiences with building VANQUISH were no different. I hate reading books written by other successful entrepreneurs and captains of industry that talk about how, one day, suddenly, the light shone on them and their respective business, and it was off to the races. Worse yet, how they went from one business venture to another and all was golden for them. My experiences tell a very different story. I am not saying they are liars. What I am saying is be prepared, because it doesn't all happen like a fairy tale. I have found that my individual life experiences are not always like living in a Hallmark Channel movie, where everything always comes together nicely. The movie scene I spend most of my day in can be easily compared to a trip on forty miles of dirt road in a 110-degree heat with a busted radiator hose. What I like to refer to as *reality!*

—————————

When I made the decision to start my own company, one of the first things I had to overcome was *fear*. The four-letter word *fear* is not that big of a word, but it conjures up images of big hairy monsters coming from under the bed to eat you alive in your sleep once the lights go out. For me, nighttime is when fear would strike. I could stay occupied through the day with activities of building the business, but once I laid my head down on the pillow, the war inside would start, and I would be up all night reliving the decisions of the day, of the week; and as business grew, the ghosts of decisions past and present would go to battle within me. Spreading their notions of doubt for the future survival of my business in my overworked brain.

I realized early on that there are many different types of fear that a new business venture forces one to deal with when the choice to start their own business is made. I identified them as three different types of fear that entrepreneurs need to learn to live with *daily*. These are, to my way of thinking, confusing and are often misinterpreted by the individual experiencing them. This confusion can lead to an overall "paralysis by analysis." I believe in a divide-and-conquer approach to dealing with fear. Which is why I think it is important to identify the three types clearly, so you can know how I dealt with them when they reared their ugly heads. Fear, in its simplest form, is good; it keeps us focused and alert. When we allow fear to overwhelm us—that is when the results can be devastating.

The first of these three fears I call the "fear of starting." Do I jump off the roof and start my own business? I call this a personal fear because it can run deep into your soul. This first fear can be overwhelming because you are contemplating upending your entire life. You are effectively putting your entire life up to this point on the line. In my case, I had two kids in school with larger-than-life tuition payments. I might be comfortable with changing my life, but I was not comfortable with changing their lives.

Second is the "decision fear." This happens daily, and in some cases, these decisions come at you rapid fire more than once a day. It is the fear that when faced with a choice—Do I stay, or do I go?—you fear making the wrong choice. In most cases these are not life-altering decisions. But the decisions do have consequences, just the same. Do I agree to take on this project? Do I have the resources, the skill set, the knowledge to accomplish what I am agreeing to, and, if so, how do I pay for it?

The third is "the fear of failure or not reaching the goal I have set for myself." This is the big one and seems to have the most consequences attached to it. If I fail, I therefore am a failure. I don't believe this statement anymore, but for new business owners, this fear can literally kill you. And that is why I am writing this chapter; I think it is that important.

To me, these three are all very real fears and need to be taken seriously. I also believe you need to learn early on how to differentiate them from each other; if you don't, they will collectively eat you alive. I contend they are all very different, and I believe most people confuse them, become overwhelmed by them and, therefore, give up on their dreams and goals when they are just about to make a breakthrough.

THE FEAR OF GETTING STARTED

I can't say I am unique or that my experiences are somehow better or worse than most. I can tell you that at age forty-two, I was given the opportunity to make a choice. The two roads had diverged in the woods, and I was faced with the personal choice of deciding which one I would walk down. Should I dust off my résumé and reinvent myself for a new employer? Or should I take the risk of reinventing myself for my own benefit?

> **The two roads had diverged in the woods, and I was faced with the personal choice of deciding which one I would walk down.**

The fear that gripped me in this moment is hard to describe in words, because it encompasses many decisions and hard choices whose outcomes are in a state of flux, consisting of variables I could not control at the time of the decision. The way I dealt with this fear was to define each choice, each decision, one at a time. On my yellow pad, I defined the choice and then defined the possible outcomes of each, good or bad. Some might call this the risk analysis method. For me, it was just a commonsense approach. I weighed the cost, not necessarily in dollars but in blood, sweat, and tears. Once I had them on paper, I could determine if I could figuratively cover the cost. Meaning that if the result was not in my favor or the outcome was not as I had intended it to be, would I be able to withstand the consequences? I have found that life is about taking risks, but not just the jumping-off-the-roof type of chances. More importantly, making sure they are calculated risks.

Every safety officer I have ever employed at VANQUISH constantly preaches to the install crews—the people in the field installing our systems in close proximately to energized electrical equipment—the need for a risk-reward assessment before every action. Is what I am about to do worth the risk? If the answer is the risk is not worth the reward, then I should not be doing it. If there is a chance that I will get hurt, then I need to find a better way to perform the task. This lesson is important in our daily lives as well as in business. If we are honest with ourselves and identify the risk-reward at these moments of decision, we will make better decisions, and by default have better consequences or results.

The saying "What doesn't kill us makes us stronger" sounds good in hindsight, but no one should take a risk if it could possibly kill them or handicap them. I have adopted the thought process that "it is better to step away from the battle and live to fight another day on a better battlefield, under more favorable circumstances, than it is to plow forward and lose it all. I did not come all this way and fight this hard to succeed only to lose it here at this moment in time." I always want to live to fight another day. It's the only way I see to accomplish my goals and to fulfill my dreams.

Don't misunderstand me; I know that in business there is truly no safety net below me, and that's the first fact to realize. As Winston Churchill said, "You have got to learn to go from failure to failure without losing your enthusiasm." Being an entrepreneur, building a business, involves taking risks. It has been said the bigger the risk, the bigger the reward, and this may be true. But a noneducated risk is not a risk worth taking, in my book. As I am fond of saying to my team, "Take educated risks, not thoughtless risks."

The way I overcame the fear of starting my own business was to first tap into the answer to the question burning deep inside of me: I needed to find my magic. Second, I did my homework. It may appear in these pages that I jumped into the deep end of the pond, but that is not true. I took the time to look around, to research, to compare, to weigh my options. I ran the final analysis through my list of rules, now known as channel markers. My new idea had to meet a strict standard before I would attempt to make it a reality. Simply put, I did the legwork by the numbers before I settled on what to do. Then, and only then, I formulated a business plan taking into consideration my four nonnegotiables.

Back to my burn-the-boats mentality. We are here to win, and if not, we leave it all on the battlefield every day. Giving it all we have here and now is the only way to win. But I assure you I do not get on the battlefield in the first place if I have not thoroughly reviewed the risks of being there, and you can be assured I have weighed the options of my strategy long before we get in the fight.

A story is told of a great warrior who approaches a fight, and fate whispers in his ear, "You cannot stand up to the storm." The warrior whispers back, "I am the storm!"

I encourage you to be the storm in your story. I am confident that is how you control the fear of getting started. I can tell you it has made all the difference for me.

THE FEAR OF MAKING WHAT APPEARS TO BE A ROUTINE DECISION

This fear can be debilitating to some. For me, not so much. I was raised by a father who loved to say "Make a decision, right, wrong, or indifferent, but make it and live with it, son!" Followed up by the statement

"Lead. Follow. Or get the hell out of the way!" I would bet money he got it from General George S. Patton, who said, "We herd sheep, we drive cattle, we lead people. Lead me, follow me, or get out of my way."

I believe this fear is the most routine one; it happens every day, and, in most cases, more than once a day. Do I buy this bolt? Do I change this design? Do I hire this individual? Do I accept this order from that customer? Simple choices and hard choices come to us every day. There are entrepreneurs who hire people to make decisions like this for them. That way they will have someone to blame if the choices don't go as planned. I have worked for people like this ... and I hated them for it. I personally had chosen to take these decisions head on for the first twelve years of VANQUISH. If I succeeded, it would be because of me. If I failed, it, too, would be because of me!

I hired a series of folks to join me at VANQUISH on the administration team. My first instructions for them were to look at what we do—and I mean everything we do. Figure out why we do it, and then make recommendations on how we could improve the processes, the products, the marketing, all the way to our interactions with the customers and potential customers.

The lesson I learned by having these innovative individuals around me was that great innovations, like great people, are not typically born; they are great because of trial and error. We must try new ideas while knowing we will fall short. I believe learning to fail and fall short means learning to get up, learn, and try again. If we don't get up, failure will be the death knell. We must learn to fail, then learn from that failing so that we don't repeat the same mistakes. Learning what *not* to do is of utmost importance if we are to learn what to do and what works best.

I have found over the years that many Christians, God-fearing individuals, use the saying "God is not finished with me yet, so be patient as I grow." I have come to modify my belief system to include that failure is healthy if I learn from it.

I firmly believe that as entrepreneurs, we need to accept the fact that we are going to fail along the way. It is an inevitable part of the formula along the path to doing our best work and ultimately achieving success. We need to allow ourselves to fail, and more importantly, we need to allow everyone on our team to understand failure is part of the process. We cannot have success if we are not free of the need for perfection. I've heard it said that we should not allow our teams to ruin the good in our effort to achieve perfection. As complicated as that sounds at first glance, if I think it through, I wholeheartedly agree.

That doesn't mean we settle for less; it means we use failure to move us forward in the process of decision-making. We risk and fail and do it with thought and learning. Because if we do not fail, we did not reach far enough to know the limits of our abilities. We must also remove the fear of failure by making it a tool by which success or the outcome we want is measured.

As individuals, we need to strive for the best. As a business team, we need to know that sometimes "good" is a step on the path to great. We cannot get too great without first trying, failing, achieving the good while striving for the best and ultimately arriving at great.

I don't believe that I need to be the smartest person in my organization. I need to hire smart people and trust them to do their job. This allows me to have multiple frames of reference in making daily decisions and overcoming the fear of making decisions. Thus, taking the teeth out of the bite of this fear of making routine decisions.

THE FEAR OF FAILURE: NOT REACHING THE GOAL I HAVE SET FOR MYSELF

I am a collector of motivational sayings, quick-witted thoughts, and poems that I read and reread during times in my life that require strength and guidance. (If you have read this far in the book, you have figured that out already, I know.) Albert Einstein is credited with having said that "I do not trouble myself with memorizing things that are easily looked up." Whether he actually said that or not is not important; what is important is the reason I keep quotes, motivational words of wit, and poems by people I respect: so that I can easily look them up and trigger the self-defense mechanism in my brain that allows me to push forward when faced with adversity. One such poem stands out for me when I am initially faced with a perceived failure. It is titled "Good Timber," by Douglas Malloch:[17]

The tree that never had to fight
For sun and sky and air and light,
But stood out in the open plain
And always got its share of rain,
Never became a forest king
But lived and died a scrubby thing.
The man who never had to toil
To gain and farm his patch of soil,
Who never had to win his share
Of sun and sky and light and air,
Never became a manly man

---

17   Douglas Malloch, *Good Timber*, https://www.familyfriendpoems.com/poem/good-timber-by-douglas-malloch.

But lived and died as he began.
Good timber does not grow with ease,
The stronger wind, the stronger trees,
The further sky, the greater length,
The more the storm, the more the strength.
By sun and cold, by rain and snow,
In trees and men good timbers grow.
Where thickest lies the forest growth
We find the patriarchs of both.
And they hold counsel with the stars
Whose broken branches show the scars
Of many winds and much of strife.
This is the common law of life.

Scrapes and cuts form the scars that make us strong. Fears and failures, tough times, and disappointments make us who we are and give us the strength and faith to know that "this, too, shall pass." The darkest nights bring the brightest days. As many a country song will say: into each life some rain shall fall. I am fully aware of the fear of failure, and you would think it would bring the biggest roadblock to success. But it is what made me feel alive. The closer I got to my dreams, the stronger the fear would seem, until I looked at it as just a part of my imagination. Much like the monsters under the bed of my youth, a simple night-light would forever destroy their control over me.

In my case, knowing I had fought the good fight, giving it all I had, made me realize that even if I failed at today's task, I had tomorrow to set the score straight again. To boil it down, I had tried so many different career paths in my life, each ending for one reason or another, and yet I never considered any of their endings a failure. Simply put, why would I let the fear of failure or failing at my own business label *me* a failure? I took away fear's power over my life simply by accepting that it was a very real possibility. However, if I fought with all I had in me, my chances of winning were greater than my chances of failing. At least to my way of thinking. I reasoned this fear away by acknowledging the fact that if I did not try, I would never know if I could have made it. And for me, the fear of not knowing was greater than the fear of failure.

CHAPTER TEN
CHANNEL MARKERS

Seek out and make teachable moments count.

As I move from being the boss, the manager of people, to being the leader of my people, my team, I need to invest in them as individuals. A large part of the investment is finding teachable moments and using those moments to educate and lead the behavior I want in my organization. I and my people need to learn to recognize those moments and to be teachable in order to grow.

I cannot let the fear of change cause me to miss an opportunity.

I have to be constantly monitoring the business climate in which VANQUISH operates so that I do not miss the market changes. I need to adapt to those changes in order to stay relevant to my customers, not only today but, more importantly, tomorrow as well. Otherwise, I may find my business going out of business. This rule was loosely inspired by Jack Welch when he said "Change before we have to."

CHAPTER ELEVEN

"Grow or Grow Faster" Is Not a Strategy

*A good plan violently executed now is better
than a perfect plan executed next week.*

—*GENERAL GEORGE PATTON*

Before COVID-19 hit the country and lockdowns became a way of life, I would annually collect my team together for a weeklong strategic planning mission. We explored where we were as a company and what our problems were and defined our goals. Then we would work together to search out solutions and opportunities for the growth of VANQUISH.

I have found that too often, CEOs and company founders like myself allow what is urgent, the day-to-day issues, to crowd out what is really important: overall growth of the company. I believe that if we are not growing as an organization, then we are dying. I have found that time invested in thoughts about the future helps us to make better decisions about what is happening today, giving us a clear understanding of where we are trying to go. Simply put, we need to know where we are trying to get to, or we will never get there.

I see strategic planning as investing in the future , and in business it cannot be overemphasized. No matter the size of the business, I

> **I see strategic planning as investing in the future.**

believe that strategy is about making specific choices to win in the marketplace. I often tell people I am not a very competitive individual. Playing board games at the dining room table I am good with winning, losing, or coming to a draw; it's just for fun. But when you move the conversation to my business focus, I am off-the-charts competitive.

In business, I believe we need a sustainable competitive advantage over our competitors. We need to deliberately choose a different set of activities designed to deliver value to our customers and ultimately to our bottom line. The strategic planning weeks were my way of investing in my team, in my business, and ultimately in my company's success in the marketplace. A. G. Lafley puts it best:[18]

> I wanted my team to understand that strategy is disciplined thinking that requires tough choices and is all about winning. Grow or grow faster is not a strategy. Build market share is not a strategy. Ten percent or greater earnings-per-share is not a strategy. Beat XYZ competitor is not a strategy. Strategy is a coordinated and integrated set of where-to-play, how-to-win, core-capability, and management system

---

18   A. G. Lafley and Roger L. Martin, *Playing to Win* (Boston: Harvard School of Business Publishing, 2013), 50.

choices that uniquely meet a consumer's needs, thereby creating competitive advantage and superior value for a business. Strategy is a way to win—and nothing less.

To Lafley's point, my team and I would spend those days hammering out the answers to the questions proposed by him. Agreeing to what would be the goals for VANQUISH and, more importantly, laying out the steps to take to make them a reality. Together, we would make the investment in time, in money, and in learning.

One of my core beliefs is that as leaders, we must mentor our team to see our vision, and together we can outline specific steps to take to win in our market. Is this a simple and cheap way to go? Not at all. The investment in time, energy, and money can be extremely expensive. But why else are we in business than to win?

Before we could be in a place with the tools to win, I needed to make the investment. And I have. And yes, I believe it is what has made all the difference for me personally, my team as individuals, and VANQUISH. Why else would all the multinational rivals in my market space come to my front door and solicit me to partner with them, and worse, offer to buy VANQUISH? I politely said, "Thank you, but no thank you." And then I would laugh. *Give it a couple more years,* I would say to myself, *and I might be offering to buy them.* In reality, I don't think that would be a good strategy, but that is a decision for my team to make.

I have found that there are levels of investment that apply to all circumstances and situations. I need to invest in research, I need to do my homework, in order to create a plan. I need to invest in myself, learn what I don't know, to become what I want to be. I need to invest in my business, giving it my time, my money, and the energy it needs to grow.

Finally, I've learned to invest in my people. While writing this book, there is a commercial on the television from the Guinness beer company. Their message is "The choices we make reveal the true nature of our character." The choices I make personally and in business do reveal, to my customers and my employees alike, the true nature of my character.

There are real and necessary levels of commitment I needed and need to make to succeed daily. I must reinforce the burn-the-boats mentality that I share with every new hire, with all in my inner circle daily, as well as with myself: We came to win, and there is not a fallback position.

To grow as a person, and for my business to grow, VANQUISH had to go where it was not comfortable and do what it did not want to do so that, in the end, we could succeed. For example, I did not want to do installations of my systems at first. Simply because I did not want the liability and responsibility that would be expected of me if I moved my company into the install business. If I am honest, I was afraid. I had been in business making a comfortable living for over thirteen years at that point, and the thought of changing what worked was not a concept I wanted to embrace.

My largest customer came to me and said that if I did not take full responsibility for a turnkey solution, they would have to limit the amount of business they could give me. A scary proposition, to say the least. At first glance, I would need to double my capital investment in equipment and double my employee count to fulfill this request. This proposition of more revenue involved more work and a larger investment, on so many levels.

I know it may sound cliché, but I have found comfort in words and quotes so many times in my life that the wisdom of Mark Twain once again rang true for me: "Do the thing you fear most, and the death of fear is certain." And "Courage is resistance to fear, mastery of fear, not absence of fear." So I dug down deep; swallowed hard, as they say; and made the investment in money, time, and energy. I bought the equipment, hired the people, and developed the install group. I won't tell you it was easy, because it was not! Frankly, it scared me, and I lost many a night's sleep as a result. But I am here today to tell you it made a difference. It more than doubled my business in terms of gross sales. In the end, the decision made VANQUISH more valuable, not only to me but to my customer base.

Being able to offer this added service to my résumé allowed new customers to take me more seriously when considering buying and using our systems. It truly set us apart from the competition, who only sold materials. I now had skin in the game, and that gave me control, ultimately allowing me to offer better products, better systems; what I learned from installing my systems allowed me to improve them. It also allowed me to better sell my systems in sales presentations because I could now speak from experience. Which in turn allowed me to make better presentations.

I wish I could tell you this was a simple decision and a simple transition for my company. But I won't lie: it was not. I once again had to rely on my faith, finding comfort in the words "Be anxious for nothing, but in everything, by prayer and supplication with thanksgiving, let our requests be made known unto God" (Philippians 4:6, NKJV).

Investing in VANQUISH, building a company, hiring employees, taking on responsibilities, satisfying a customer; the process has taught me a lot. I have tried to outline the lessons I have learned here in this book, and I would be remiss if I did not share the lesson that has meant all the difference.

There is a distinction between being a leader and being a boss. Both are based on authority, but to quote Klaus Balkenhol, a German equestrian and Olympic champion, "A boss demands blind obedience; a leader earns his authority through understanding and trust."

If we are to build a team—and I believe you can only succeed in business if you have a team to support you, your dreams, and your goals—the lesson to be learned is to move on from the idea that you are the boss and what you say goes, even if it is wrong. The bigger challenge is that you are to be a leader who shares a vision and a belief while mentoring your team to success.

Jack Welch puts it this way:[19]

When you are a leader, your job is to have all the questions. You have to be incredibly comfortable looking like the dumbest person in the room. Every conversation you have about a decision, a proposal, or a piece of market information has to be filled with you saying, "What if?" and "Why not?" and "How come?"

In the same vein, my hero Jim Collins states that[20]

those who build great companies understand that the ultimate throttle on growth for any great company is not markets, or technology, or competition, or products. It is

---

19 Jack Welch, *Winning* (New York City: Harper Collins, 2009).

20 Jim Collins, *Good to Great* (New York City: Harper Business, 2001), 54.

one thing above all others: the ability to get and keep enough of the right people.

In addition, my faith tells me that

whoever walks with the wise become wise, but the companion of fools will suffer harm (Proverbs 13:20, NKJV).

Combine all these postulations, and the lesson I have learned is that I cannot just be the boss simply because I made the biggest investment in terms of money and time. I must be the leader. And to be a great leader, I need to ask questions! I need to become comfortable not having all the answers but to be powerful in the knowledge that I have asked the right questions that will

> **To be a great leader, I need to ask questions!**

allow my team to collectively arrive at the ideal answers. Together, we will coalesce around the right direction in which to proceed and formulate the right action to take in any given situation. Allowing us and VANQUISH to act, learn from that action, revise our approach, and to act again. Thus ultimately achieving preeminent success, which will afford my team and me the ability to do the things that others won't so we can continue to do the things they can't.

In the spring of 2017, I purchased a pair of motorcycles. When we are young, we have ideas about what we want and what is important to us. Then life sets in, and our responsibilities force us to put some dreams and goals on hold. Owning a motorcycle was one of those dreams for me for a host of reasons. Suffice to say that in 2017 I was in a spot to revive this desire, and I bought two bikes. One resides in Pennsylvania and one in North Carolina, the two places I spend most of my time these days. My good friend Bob Katzmar, whom I believe learned to ride before he could walk, taught me to ride. The one lesson he worked tirelessly to impress upon me was look where you want to go, not where you are going; ultimately, that is where the bike will go. Look where you want to go, not where you are going! Good advice, if you follow it.

On Saturday, April 2, 2022, almost five years to the day of buying the bikes, I was on a ride with some friends in North Carolina. It was a beautiful spring afternoon, and we were riding the curves of a beautiful backcountry winding road. A rider's dream ride. As the turns in the road got progressively tighter, I found myself slipping closer to the right side of the pavement than I should. When it became clear to me that I was not going to make the turn, I made the rookie mistake of looking off the road into the soft shoulder. True to the rule Bob taught me, I went where I was looking instead of where I wanted to go. Off the pavement I went! I rode the rough shoulder along the edge of the blacktop for a bit, but as the bike tire caught the edge of the road surface, the bike turned abruptly back to the left and laid me down hard on the asphalt surface of the road. I flew off the bike and bounced hard on my right shoulder, breaking my collarbone, my shoulder (in two places), eight ribs, and five vertebrae, and I punctured my right lung.

The point I am making is that just as it goes for riding a motorcycle, it goes for living life. And so it goes in business. Look where you want to go, not where you are going, or you will never get there—and worse, you can get seriously hurt. I will recover from these injuries, but it would have been a lot smarter if I did not end up with them in the first place.

Leaving JAGFN was a result of the impending end of the dot-com bubble, which gave me a front-row seat to the carnage and the cold reality of being collateral damage. The lessons I learned in the years after were clearly defined in *Zero to One*, where Thiel states there were four big lessons learned from the dot-com crash that still guide business thinking today:

- Make incremental advances

- Stay lean and flexible

- Improve on the competition

- Focus on product, not sales

Thiel's book was written in 2014. Fortunately, in the early days of creating my business, I had instinctively learned and incorporated the basics of these four bullet points in "Don's rules to live by in life and business." When I read Thiel's book, it felt good that he'd confirmed what I thought and what I operated my business by. And as such, I am compelled to share my interpretation here in these pages.

1. Start your business with one clear underlying idea for a product or a service, and make it or do it the best you possibly can from day one.

Strive to make small changes and advances to enhance your offering as you go. All the while keeping your focus on improving what is working and eliminating or replacing what is not working to your satisfaction. Don't attempt to conquer the world in the first battle. Take incremental steps to change. For me, this meant starting with a quality product, studying its effectiveness, and modifying small areas with each install.

2. Keep your company lean and flexible.

I believe a good plan violently executed today is better than a perfect plan executed next week. Having a plan is extremely important. The old adage "failing to plan is planning to fail" holds true in life and, more importantly, in business. You must have a defined set of goals and an outline of the steps necessary to achieve those goals. Be sure to keep the head count to the exact number of individuals and talents necessary to operate efficiently with an eye toward flexibility. Always be ready to change direction should circumstance dictate.

3. Don't reinvent the mousetrap; build a better mousetrap.

Build your business based on improving on or solving a clear and identifiable problem for an established customer. Offer a solution to a recognized problem that is in search of a solution. Build your business in a market that is already willing to spend budgeted dollars in a search for your answer. Don't try to create a new market for your product right out of the starting gate. Build a following before you try to create your own market.

4. Focus on the product or service; the quality of what you are selling should be second to none and should be your primary goal. Don't start with the focus on sales; sales will come if what you offer is worth the purchase price to the customer.

It is my belief that I need to put quality first, and the sales will take care of themselves. To paraphrase Thiel's words: if your product requires advertising to sell it, it's not good enough. I believe if you have to be constantly closing, you do not have a good enough product or service.

To bring the strategic planning requirements of VANQUISH full circle, we need to accept that strategic planning is a disciplined way of thinking that, if done right, requires tough choices to be made. If we are to be successful, we need to decide how we are going to create a competitive advantage and superior value for our business. We offer specialized systems to protect electric utility assets. We win by supplying quality solutions that are complete systems that work. Our core capability is that we have been solving out-of-the-norm problems for the industry for over twenty years; we *listen and solve* as opposed to *solve and tell*. Our management has implemented a system of choices that meet our customers' needs every day.

Back to General George Patton's quote that opened this chapter, we need to see our strategy as a way to win—and nothing less. We are executing a good plan violently now and working, at the same time, on a perfect plan to be executed next week!

CHAPTER ELEVEN
CHANNEL MARKERS

Invest in my people.

Think in the "we" mindset, not in the "I" mindset. I believed, from the start, that "I" was a "we" and that "we" would be a team at VANQUISH one day. Once I started to invite people to play in my sandbox, I needed to have a way to invest in them so that each person could be as productive as possible. At first this investment was their paychecks. But in short order, it became an investment in education and, to a larger degree, an investment of my time to coach and lead them to productivity.

Make the investment to win.

I believed that I needed to make specific choices to win in the marketplace. A. G. Lafley, former chairman and CEO of Procter & Gamble, along with Roger L. Martin, dean of the Rotman School of Management, said it best in their book *Playing to Win*: "A company must seek to win in a particular place and in a particular way. If it doesn't seek to win, it is wasting the time of its people and the investments of its capital provider."[21] In the case of VANQUISH, it is my capital. By making this one of my rules, I chose to make the investment to win.

Make incremental advances.

As my product line advanced, I would continually study its effectiveness, and as necessary I made continuous improvements to the actual product and the way I presented it. Basically, I tweaked every aspect of

---

21   A. G. Lafley and Roger L. Martin, *Playing to Win*, 19.

my service, my products, and my business to be sure they were all the very best they could be based on the knowledge I had at that moment in time. Once I had better data, I improved continually based on that new knowledge.

Look where I want to go, not where I am going.

Regardless of where business is today, I find that, just like riding my motorcycle, I need to look where I want my business to go: in the direction of my goals. In doing so, my team and I will make decisions today that will ultimately lead the business toward the achievement of those goals in the future.

CHAPTER TWELVE

Always Trust Your Cape!

And I say onto you, ask, and it shall be given you; seek,
and ye shall find; knock, and it shall be opened unto you.
For everyone that asketh receiveth; and he that seeketh
findeth; and to him that knocketh it shall be opened.

—2 CORINTHIANS 13:14

By now you are well aware that I have always referred to the "we" of VANQUISH, even in the earlier years of my business, long before I had an actual team to work with, I would say "we" did this or "we" can make that change or "we" should consider incorporating that into our system. I remember one day, long ago, I was talking with my father about the current happenings at VANQUISH, and after some time he looked at me and said, "Do you have a mouse in your pocket? Who is this 'we' you keep talking about?"

At the time I did not have a good answer for him other than to say "I will be a 'we' someday, and I am speaking that desire into existence by putting it out in the universe today." Then I came across Peter Drucker's quote, and my natural way of thinking suddenly made sense:[22]

> The leaders who work most effectively it seems to me, never say "I." And that's not because they have trained themselves not to say "I." They don't think "I." They think "we": they think "team." They understand their job to be to make the team function. They accept responsibility and don't sidestep it, but "we" gets the credit. This is what creates trust, what enables you to get the task done.

I watched a show on the Discovery Channel that showed how, in the beginning, when man was a hunter and gatherer, he would run through the woods with his spear, knife, bow and arrows, or slingshot, chasing animals to kill for his and his family's dinner. Surely a tough way to survive. In our innate desire to survive and thrive, we all need to provide for ourselves and our families. What I learned about these early men is they soon started to observe, to study their prey; and instead of running off to chase them, they recognized patterns in the behavior of the animals they were hunting.

I believe I've been fortunate enough to live the life I have because I have learned to have the desire to control my own destiny so that no one else does.

---

22   Peter Drucker, "Peter Drucker on Leadership," The Leadersmith, accessed January 31, 2023, https://www.daringerdes.com/peter-drucker-on-leadership/.

They learned that the prey would eventually find its way to water. These primitive men began to set up near the watering hole, and the animals they desired and so desperately needed would come to them.

I believe I've been fortunate enough to live the life I have because I have learned to have the desire to control my own destiny so that no one else does. When I was technically a self-employed contractor at Prudential Securities in the early days of my career, my manager would love to come into my office and tell me what he thought I should be doing with my time. I would listen and then say, "Is this a condition of employment? Because if it is, I quit." This simple statement would drive him crazy, and he would storm out of my office in disgust. It is this attitude of mine that I am sure was the basis of me wanting to control my own future, my own destiny.

I promise I was not born rich. In fact, until I was in the tenth grade, my dad was a hardworking truck driver, and my mom was a front desk clerk at the local Hopewell Valley newspaper. I don't believe I had any greater chances than the average person. What I did have was the belief that I could personally make it happen. Even though it took me twenty years to figure what to do, and another twenty years to make it happen, it was not only worth it, but it was also one of the best things I ever did for myself and my family.

In the last week of January 2021—after barely holding my business together through the COVID-19 pandemic that held all of 2020 hostage with its lockdowns and quarantine restrictions—my largest customer informed me that they were postponing all capital projects until 2022. The result of which was the hard, cold reality that I would need to drastically downsize VANQUISH just to survive.

In the same week, my youngest brother passed away suddenly at the age of fifty-seven. Two days later, my mom passed away. She was alone, because of COVID-19 restrictions, in a hospital bed in Florida. If ever there were a time and circumstance great enough to cause a man to crumple and quit, this would surely be one of them.

I could have felt sorry for myself, and no one would have blamed me. The line "At least we had our chances" would have been a fitting epitaph, if I had chosen to stop. But the desire that burned in me would not let this unfortunate set of circumstances control me or my emotions. I am not saying it was easy; I assure you, it was not! Everything I had ever read, ever learned, ever put my faith in: my moral fabric would not rip. When you are faced with the reality that you have lost something that you can't replace, when the tears stream down your face—this is the time you must get up and try again! It has been said that these are the moments when you see just how great you can be. You must try to fix it. If I didn't believe it before, I did now. As the boxer Mike Tyson once said, "Everyone has a plan until they get punched in the mouth." I felt that week as if I had truly been punched in the mouth so very unexpectedly.

I assure you, I do not consider myself a great man. But I knew this was the time when great men, above all others, define the difference between success and failure as the great divide to be crossed. I had to believe. I needed to be passionate once again. So many people depended on me and needed me to be the leader I professed to be. I believed I needed to be the phoenix that rose from the ashes. Not just for them but for me.

I needed to act immediately. I had read all the books. And I believed in them as I built the business and applied all the lessons to great success up to this point, I'd reasoned. If so, I needed to believe in them now and make the changes called for to survive and rise again.

I knew what had to be done, and now more than ever, I needed to summon the courage to do it.

When people ask how you knew what to do and how you did it so swiftly when faced with such devastation, I believe that, like all successful athletes, we as entrepreneurs need to develop our muscle memory. A concept not often heard of in business. We as leaders need to practice every day what we have learned. We need to prepare ourselves for the day when we do not have time to think; we need to react and to be able to trust our reaction is the right one. That comfort level can only come from having practiced, having prepared, in advance of the day. Just like the great golfers, basketball players, and any other great athletes, we need to trust that when we call on our muscles to react in the heat of the moment, they will respond as we practiced. I cannot overemphasize the fact that our brains and our muscles must be ready to act when action is required. There is no time to think when our emotions are running so strong; we need to be in a place where we react and react rightly.

I am not overstating it when I tell you that by Friday of that horrible week in January, I had lived through one of the toughest periods of my life and my business life as they both converged on me. I laid off half my staff. I reduced my overhead. I began the process of selling off assets to reduce my costs. I applied for and received all the Paycheck Protection Program money the government's Small Business Administration (SBA) had to offer. I turned all the debt on my balance sheet into a loan from the SBA. I stopped my pay, my 401(k) contributions, and my educational fund deposits for my grandchildren for the next year and a half. I reinvested every dime saved back into the business. I worked with my team to refocus our efforts for sales and new customer acquisitions. I worked with my chief operating officer to encourage a small group of outside investors to loan us funds to keep the ship afloat in the short term. My actions during this time were contagious. The belief in the return to greatness was a plan I put into place with my team. I defined this as a short-term problem and not a fatal flaw in our business model.

I presented my team with an adaptation of Jack Welch's six rules—something that I had created for myself years ago—and we continue to focus all our efforts on them:

- Face reality as it is, not as it was or as we wish it were.

- Be candid with everyone.

- Don't manage; lead.

- Change before we have to.

- If we don't have a competitive advantage, don't compete.

- Control our own destiny, or someone else will.

I also reminded them of the fact that we had adapted the following mindset years ago: Every Day We Make It, We Will Make It the Best We Can. I felt it was appropriate for us as a team to keep this in the front of our thoughts at this moment in time.

I do not profess to be a hero. But the actions we each took personally and as a company allowed us to survive through the rest of 2021. By the following January, almost a year to the week, we were reaping the rewards of our efforts. We now had a much leaner organization. Jim Collins would be proud! We would be great again. The right people on the bus and in the right seats, as he would say. We were an engine functioning, I believe, on all cylinders. Each department was focused and producing. The workload was slowly returning, and the downcycle we had just gone through gave us clarity for the future and how we fit into it. I can honestly say I never want to live through another two years like we had just gone through, but it did prove to be a necessary cleansing of the organization.

My message had now changed, and I had a renewed faith that VANQUISH would survive and that we were once again in the sweet spot of life. I became fond of singing my own version of Bruno Mars's lyrics around the office: "It's Saturday night, and we are in the spot. If you don't believe me, just watch!"

What we had just gone through could be described as having gone through the fire and being refined into fine silver or gold. Or as Kevin Eastman stated in his book, *Why the Best are the Best*, "The three dimensions of success. We had learned from the past—produced in the present—and—prepared for the future."[23]

We at VANQUISH were now better prepared for the future. In fact, from where I sat at that moment, we were about to be overloaded with work. The time without our largest customer online allowed us to expand our customer base beyond them. In doing so, we reduced our dependency on that customer to a point that, if we have done our homework and planned properly for the future, our decisions and strategy will make us stronger. We have reduced our dependence on them to the point that if they pull back again, we should not get hurt as bad.

This change in business philosophy reminds me of a favorite Bible verse: "Therefore, said he unto them, the harvest truly is great, but the laborers are few; pray ye, therefore the Lord of the harvest, that he would send forth laborers into his harvest" (Luke 10:2).

---

23   Kevin Eastman, *Why the Best Are the Best* (Charleston: Advantage Media Group, 2018), 142.

A few months later, I returned to my home in Pennsylvania, and my wife said to me, "What's wrong? You look like you've got something on your mind." I paused, then said to her that at that moment in time, things were good. Really good. We had plenty of work. We had money in the bank. We had new customers. The organization was as lean as it could be. Everyone was getting along. The future looked bright. Yet she was right—something was off. And then it dawned on me ... we were free floating.

At that exact point in time, the business, and I personally, did not have any resistance. We had what I would call normal day-to-day issues. But no major problems. For the first time in a long time, there was nothing pushing back on me.

The best way I can describe this is when you work with weights in a gym, you want resistance to grow the muscles. But when your muscles grow to the point that the weight offers no resistance, it is time to up the weights. That moment of no resistance was, and is, for me, disconcerting. As a CEO, you want your business constantly pushing up the hill, feeling the resistance. That is how you know you are moving in the right direction. After all, if it were easy, everyone would be doing it.

> **If it were easy, everyone would be doing it.**

I reasoned that it must be time to gather my management team together and have a strategic planning session to look at the future. To create challenges for ourselves. To drive us to greater heights and levels of growth. To create some resistance. And in the spirit of Guy Clark's song, we need to wrap the flower sack cape around our necks and take a leap of faith ...

... and to once again, Trust Our Cape!

CHAPTER TWELVE
CHANNEL MARKERS

It is more important for me to be a great leader than it is to be a great boss.

I need to be the visionary and the keeper of the dream and to lead my team to take us in the direction of change and growth if VANQUISH is to survive and thrive. This rule was loosely inspired by Jack Welch, who is reported to preach that as a leader, I needed to be powerful in the knowledge that I have asked the right questions of my team.

Leave my ego at the door.

I have observed that some entrepreneurs get to a point where they believe they know more than anyone else and that they are somehow smarter than the rest. To my way of thinking, this is a very dangerous position to be in. Therefore I need to leave my ego at the door and learn to listen as well as hear.

The right people are my most important asset.

This rule is based on the principles I learned from Jim Collins in *Good to Great*, in which he talks about Level 5 leaders and the importance of having the right people on the bus, and in the right seats, before you decide where to drive the bus.

Practice intellectual honesty.

This rule came to me via Peter Drucker, a management consultant, educator, and author, whose writings contributed to the philosophical and practical foundations of modern business. Combined with Jack

Welch's "Reality Principle," they form the basis of teams working together for the greater good of the business. Our management team members must be honest with each other and trust each other if they are to lead the organization to greater success.

Be candid with everyone.

This flows out of the "Practice intellectual honesty" rule. Management must be candid and honest with each other if they are to create harmony within the organization.

Don't manage; lead.

In order for my business to grow, I need to be the visionary, the leader, the one who speaks inspiration into the mission of my company. Therefore I need to lead my team to determine the means to success. I cannot manage them to success.

Face reality as it is, not as it was or as I wish it were.

This rule was also inspired by Jack Welch and my dad. Both men harped on living in the reality of things. My dad would say, "Don't feel sorry for yourself, son; get up, face reality, deal with it." I have now and forever adapted that attitude in life and in business. I cannot make choices for my business based on what I would like to see in the real world. I need to make choices on what I know to be real in the world today.

I need to build my entrepreneurial muscle memory every day so that when I need it I will not have to stop to think. I will instinctively act.

Watch athletes, especially great ones. They practice for hours, repeating the same action over and over again, building what they call *muscle memory*. When in a game and the moment comes to take the shot or make the throw, they don't think; they just act. I believe that as a leader of my business, I need to practice every day so that when the time comes I know how to respond. I need to build my muscle memory, just like the athletes.

Resistance is needed to grow.

I have found that just like weightlifters in the gym, I need to feel resistance when working out to grow my "business" muscles. My business and my leadership team need to feel the wind in our faces, pushing back, in order to keep us sharp, growing, and focused and to know we are going in the right direction. When the wind is always at our back, we have a tendency to become weak and to lose focus on the goal.

Bonus rule: I must believe in myself and my abilities.

Or put another way: *Always Trust Your Cape!*

The Possibilities Are Truly Limitless

I'm a success today because I had a mom who believed
in me, and I didn't have the heart to let her down.

—*DONALD E. MOORE*

The opening quote is my take on one of my most favorite quotes of all time. That is saying something, because, as you can tell from reading this book, I have so many quotes that I love and keep close at hand. It was originally said by Abraham Lincoln: "I'm a success today because I had a friend who believed in me, and I didn't have the heart to let him down."

Mr. Lincoln is one of those people who, given the chance, I would love to have dinner with. I find him fascinating on so many levels. He came from the humblest of beginnings, and even though he reached unbelievable success in his short life, he stayed humble as the world around him crumbled. Not to mention he led my country through some of the darkest days of its existence.

I have taken the liberty here to change the focus of this quote as I attribute it to my mom. She did not ever think of any of her sacrifices as anything other than what a mom does for her children. I told her many times I was grateful she decided at such a young age to give birth to me, and she would just smile.

My mom truly believed in me and whatever career path I was on at any given time throughout my life. She and I found Jesus together, and she helped foster my growth as a human and a man. She lived part of her life vicariously through my success, I am sure. I remember how much joy it gave her to see my family grow; to meet my children, Ashley and Brandon; and to hear of the successes they and VANQUISH, my third child, and I were having at any given moment in time. I have so many memories of her and the times in my life that can only be appreciated through a mother's eyes. I know I will see her again, and for that I cannot wait.

Of all the important women in my life, my mom and my wife, Christina, are two whom I could not afford to let down. They both believed in me and gave me, in their own way, the space and encouragement to be what I would call *successful*. I like to believe I made them both proud.

When people learn of the success of VANQUISH, they inevitably tell me how lucky or how blessed I am to have a successful business. Some go so far as to say "God has truly blessed you; you are so lucky." In response, I tell them a story (or at least I tell it to anyone who will listen):[24]

---

24   Author unknown.

There once was a new minister in town, and he made it a practice of riding around town to introduce himself and to invite people to come to his church on Sunday. One day he stopped in front of the most beautiful farm. The barns and house were painted and landscaped. The fences were mended and painted, and the fields were fertile with crops planted and growing. The livestock was healthy and grazing in the greenest of pastures. The minister noticed the farmer plowing a field, and so he stood by the fence along the road and waited for the farmer to circle around and come near the fence line. The farmer approached and turned off the tractor to acknowledge the minister. Greetings and introductions were exchanged. The minister could not contain himself, and he said that the farm was by far the most beautiful he had ever seen. The farmer smiled as the minister said "You should be proud the Lord has blessed you with such a wonderful farm." The farmer was taken aback slightly, thought for a moment, and replied. "Yes, but you should have seen the place when the Lord had it by himself!"

My point in telling this story is that today, when people visit VANQUISH and they see our facilities, our buildings, our warehouses, our furnished and decorated offices, our fabrication facilities with floors you could eat off of, and the condition of our equipment, they inevitably say the same thing to me over and over: "You are blessed. God has truly shined his light on you and your business."

> **I believe the journey is worth the price for making your dream come true.**

ALWAYS TRUST YOUR CAPE

I reply, "Yes! But you should have seen it when the Lord had it all by himself!"

Now, I mean no slight or disrespect here; it is just that I have worked very hard to have what I have and to build what I have built in my life and in VANQUISH. I know that it can all be gone in a blink of an eye. And yes, I had help, but I worked very hard and very long hours to build what I would call my success. As you can tell, I am very proud of what I have accomplished. It is for this reason that I wanted this book to be an encouragement to the reader. It can be done. It does come at a cost. Don't underestimate that cost when you start this journey. But know this: I believe the journey is worth the price for making your dream come true.

It's been said that everyone wants to eat, but few are willing to hunt. The purpose of writing this book is to dispense a lesson or two I believe are worth sharing. My motive is simple: to encourage someone—you, perhaps—to step out and build a dream. To start a business and to take comfort in the knowledge of learning what I did and what guided me through the highs and lows of building my dream. To that end, I believe you have got to be willing to hunt. To get up each day with the drive and the burning desire to do whatever it takes to make that dream a reality. Because in the end, you are the only one who can do that for yourself.

My friend and my chief operating officer at VANQUISH, Steve Schoepfer—the same person who was my boss all those years ago at JAGFN on that fateful day when, for me, two roads diverged in the woods—has been in my life since the days when we met some thirty years ago at Prudential Securities in Princeton, New Jersey. We were in the trenches together in those days, and we had a motto: we only get to eat today what we kill. The lesson to be learned is that you must be willing to hunt to succeed. It is not easy, I assure you. But it is my sincere hope that the pages of this book have inspired you, that I have opened your eyes to the struggles, the defeats, that run alongside the moments of great joy that you can experience in your endeavor. I pray that I have left you with a hunger deep inside you and that the hunger will drive you to hunt. Because it is only you who can make your dream come alive and become real.

Peter Drucker once said, "Whenever you see a successful business, someone once made a courageous decision." That decision is not one to take lightly. It takes courage and tenacity. While it is true that the possibilities are truly limitless, you must be willing. I hope this book inspires you to be prepared and to take the chance on yourself. If you have a dream, then chase it. Because that dream is not going to chase you back.

I say to you now, spread your arms and hold your breath … and *always* trust your cape!

AFTERWORD

While my story continues, I wrote this book for one other slightly selfish reason. I wanted it to be a love letter to my grandchildren and the future generations that will follow me in this life. I wanted to give them a window into the past and who I was, how I lived, and what I believed.

Today, I see all these folks working with companies like Ancestry. com, trying to piece together past relatives and family lines in hopes of finding some bit of information about themselves. If I have done it right, this book is my gift to each of my relatives, known and unknown. I leave you, and them, with what I believe is the true fountain of youth, which to my way of thinking is summed up in three lines: have faith to forget the past, have faith to face the facts, and most of all, have the faith to face the future.

I encourage you to take comfort, as I do, in knowing that it is my expectations for the future that guide my steps, the planting of seeds today, so that I am in a position to reap the rewards of tomorrow!

ACKNOWLEDGMENTS

I find it nearly impossible to look back over my life and give a full accounting for the reasons why so many people took the time and interest to help and guide me on my journey. It's even harder to identify the moments they shared with me leading up to the writing of this book. But I would be remiss if I did not at least try to thank those who have helped me along the way. For those I list below and those whose names are lost to me now, I want you to know I consider myself to be a blessed individual for having crossed paths with you. My strength in the Lord was given to me by each of you angels, who spoke your wisdom and your criticisms into my ear and my life.

Alberta Moore, my mom, one of the strongest women I have ever known; she taught me to love life by giving me life. She ingrained in me from the start the idea that life is a gift, and that I should live it to the fullest every day. She fostered in me the desire to never be afraid to try new things. She made me believe I could fly. She taught me to trust in the Lord and to be the best I could be and, more importantly, to never live in the past. I did my best, Mom!

The women in my life, truly God's gifts to me: Christina, my wife and partner of forty years; Ashley, my daughter, my idol; Sue and Alicia, my sisters, my cheering section. Together, their love and adoration has kept my spirit strong through the good and bad times along this path in the woods I decided to travel down.

Jackilyn VanOpdorp, my niece, thank you for believing in my passion. In recent years, I have come to appreciate your direction, strategy, and friendship. Your unrelenting push for perfection has truly elevated the VANQUISH brand. Your vision and your ability to keep me always focused on the reality of things has become something I depend on daily. My story would not be the same without your undying enthusiasm and can-do attitude.

Veronica Birardi, my niece, for your trust, your love, and your ability to let me see the world through your rose-colored glasses for a time. You are truly one of life's flowers along this road less traveled that I am on. I look forward to the day you grace my doorstep again as your passion for life is sorely missed in the halls of VANQUISH. Thank you for sharing the most special part of you with me.

Steve Falcone, my friend, my accountant, one of my trusted advisors, it is you who have been my guide and a steady voice of reason, through this roller coaster of a ride I have been on for over thirty years now. Your wisdom and loyalty are second to none and one of the biggest reasons I survived at this business called VANQUISH all these years. You and your silent team are greatly appreciated!

Steve Schoepfer, you started this walk, this journey with me from the beginning. You taught me that everyone wants to eat but so few want to hunt. Both physically and in spirit, we are now consumed by the fire that is VANQUISH. The truth be told, I cannot think of anyone I would rather have in the lifeboat rowing with me than you. Your unlimited kindness and enthusiasm toward the cause, long before there was a cause, is the foundation upon which VANQUISH is built. Thank you for your loyalty and dedication. I am proud to call you my friend.

Donna Kates, Kim Ray, Debbie Sobon, Meghan Jones, Jenna Frank, and Lynne Rostock, without each of your talents, VANQUISH might have been a dream that died along the way. I thank you for your love, your support, your guidance, and your strength. Without each of you in your own time, this journey would have been a whole lot harder than it was. I love you all!

Emma Moore and Mildred Bonura, my grandmothers, who loved me unconditionally and, in so doing, taught me that doing without, living simply, for so long was not "suffering," to their way of thinking. They taught me to be humble and thankful just by living their lives. I am thankful I was the oldest grandchild, as I got to spend time with them and got to know them in ways my siblings did not.

Donald Brandon Moore, my son, the architect, the cornerstone in the building that is my life. It is you who holds the time capsule of all that I am, all that I strive to build, and all that I leave behind for those who come after me. You are truly one of my life's greatest accomplishments!

Donald G. Moore, my father, one of the toughest men I have ever known. Your lessons for life and business were thrust on me by force. Cementing in my foundation as a man, as a father, as a husband, the commitment to do something different with my life and to do it better than even I thought possible. I took your advice and separated the good from the bad, and that has made all the difference.

Steve, my son-in-law, the teacher, and the father of my two unbelievable granddaughters, thank you for listening to my stories. George Forrest, for pointing me in the direction of animal deterrent and telling me to think outside of the box all those years ago.

Samuel Eugene Bonura, my grandfather, my mom's dad. We called him Poppy, a name I have taken on in my role as a grandfather. You bonded with me from birth, and it was your view of me that I treasured most. You had no sons, and I believe God gave you to me so I could see the softer side of what it was to be a man. Thank you for staying with us for as long as you could.

George "Chubby" Moore, my grandfather, my dad's dad, thank you for sharing your stories. In doing so, you showed me how tough life can be, and how many scars we humans must learn to live with on our journey. You survived all that life gave you, and in your setbacks and your successes that you experienced as a young man, you taught me that life may not be fair, but it is still my life to live, and it will be what I make it.

The men in my life and business, my support system: Tim Mooney, Brian VanDyke, Charles Strickland, Neil Grogan, Earl Coble, Sean Flanagan, Michael Heine, and Tom Mazzarisi. You each have played your own unique role in the building of VANQUISH. Thank you for sticking with me through the years, especially when times got tough! This book and its stories would not be possible without you all.

Robert Katzmar, truly a man above all others, you fostered my growth. You were a landlord, an employee, a mentor, a guide, a teacher, and a loyal friend. You treated me like family, and for that I am grateful. You reawakened a love of motorcycles I forgot I had. Because of you, I found peace and harmony in life by riding. Even if it almost killed me. Thank you.

Mr. Raymond Cox, my first true friend when we moved to the town of Hopewell, who took the time to mentor a young twelve-year-old boy. Above all, you taught me to look at the world around me and to really try to see it and its opportunities. Just as importantly, you taught me to love the smell and taste of a good cigar. May you rest in peace, my friend.

To the men of my youth whose first names I never knew, because in those days we did not call adults by their first name. They were always and forever will be Mr. Pullen, the Baptist minister who baptized my mom and me. Mr. Dansbury, a deacon at the church, who taught me about small-town politics. Mr. Clayton, my high school drawing teacher, who taught me the principle of corrective criticism. Mr. Sheetz, my eighth-grade vice-principle and history teacher, for explaining to me how to grow up and be a leader. Mr. Holcombe, my eighth-grade track coach, for teaching me how to push through the pain. Mr. Wright and Mr. Hill, owners of the Hopewell Lumber Yard, who gave me my first charge account at the age of thirteen, thank you for trusting me. Mr. Conrad, the owner of the bike store in Pennington, New Jersey, thank you for teaching me how to run a bicycle repair shop. Mr. Macintosh, owner of the Hopewell Upholstery Company, for your insight into service and for mentioning that you were an MP in the army all those years ago. Mr. Flynn, the owner of Pennington Hardware, and Mr. Richard, owner of the *Hopewell Valley News*. Each of these men gave me a taste of responsibility and humility and, in some cases, gave me my first jobs while investing time into me at an age when role models were so influential to becoming an adult who could function in the real world. Thank you.

Keith Wycoff, my high school friend, two years my senior, the older brother in my younger life, who taught me about paper routes and how to repair bicycles. You planted the seeds that eventually grew into the love of business and capitalism all those years ago. I trust your success all these years has done you well.

Jack McKenzie, my adopted uncle and my father's business partner. Thank you for your love, your guidance, and all the Saturdays you took me bowling. You showed me the softer side of life, and for that I am forever grateful. You left us far too soon, and you are missed.

Mark Pelicone, my closest of friends, my confidant. There is no doubt that if I had partnered with anyone when the two roads diverged in the woods, you would have been half owner of VANQUISH. You knew the dream was there inside me, and you saw it more clearly than I could. Unfortunately for me, God had other plans and took you long before your time. I miss you, my friend.

Mr. Jimmy Reed, my high school algebra teacher who stayed after class every day for a semester, my senior year, to tutor me. I am not sure why you did it, but I am forever thankful that you did.

Mr. Magnavitta, my college algebra professor, you showed me that I could not only understand advanced mathematics, but I could also grow to love it! More importantly you instilled in me the notion that if I want it bad enough and worked hard enough, I could actually achieve it, with great success. You single-handedly are why I finished my college education. Thank you.

Roger Hicks, the junkyard dog of a friend who hated me when we first met our senior year in high school. The best man at my wedding. Thank you for the opportunity you gave me to broaden my horizons. You allowed me to do something I never thought I could do—work on Wall Street. Thank you for pushing me off the cliff into the abyss, where I found something even better.

Larry Vise, one of life's many guides, the man who has forgotten more about fences and what it takes to build a business than I will ever know. Thank you for investing in me. For traveling with me. For showing me how to flip ideas on their side and use them in ways not thought of before. You introduced me to people, vendors, and ideas I might never have thought of on my own. You have taught me so much, and I am forever grateful!

My brothers, Ed and Tom, who, for the most part, were my complete opposites and who followed in Dad's footsteps in business and beliefs. And in so doing, by your choices, you taught me it was okay to become "the odd duck" of the family. By your actions, you taught me a thing or two about life and opened my eyes to the reasons it was necessary to take the opportunities when they came, which led me down the road less traveled when faced with the choice.

Mario Birardi, Christina's dad, my father-in-law, a man who believed in me, supported me, respected me, and in so doing, taught me how to be a good father-in-law to Ashley's husband. You did not live long enough to see my success, but I think you already knew it was inevitable, even if I had doubts back then.

My clients, for trusting me and allowing me the opportunity to prove to the world there is a safe way to effectively protect substation assets in a humane and community-acceptable way. While affording me the ability to live my dream of building my brand and my own company every day. This book is the consequence of all our hard work together. Thank you.

Jim Collins, a man I never met, the author of many books I find inspirational. Thank you for teaching me by your amazing work: the concept of the flywheel effect, your research on core values and core purpose, and most importantly, for enlightening me on the need for putting the right people, Level 5 leaders, on the bus and in the right seats. Even though you may never know, you have guided every step I have taken in business. You have truly changed the course of business for me and countless others. To you, I say a huge thank-you!

Simon Presland, who sat with me through the process of putting this story on paper. You helped me see my thoughts and ideas through the eyes of the reader. I can honestly say this book would not have gotten written if you were not my guide. Thank you.

The people who were in the picture frame of life and business for a short period and, for one reason or another, are now onto other endeavors. Scott Reeder, Jim Wilson, Eric Linker, Jerry Allen, Lenard Anderson, Bill Breedlove, David Hansil, Tony Birardi, Mario M.

Birardi, Teresa VanDyke, German Alverez, Wayne Hatley, and Ms. Lee Hancock: each of you have left your mark on VANQUISH and me personally. Thank you.

Finally, but not last by any means, thank you to my Lord Jesus Christ, who gave me this unbelievable opportunity to serve.

I know it goes that I have forgotten someone, and for that I am truly sorry. It is not that your contribution to my life was not important or memorable; it is just that I am getting old. So please know in my heart you are appreciated and loved, even if I failed to mention you by name. Hear me now when I say "Thank you!"

RECOMMENDED BOOKS

Ashley, my daughter, the communications expert in my life, once told me that as a CEO, I needed to have a list of books that, when asked, I could share or recommend to my staff, my team, and those I interact with daily to allow them to gain a perception on me and my thought process or belief system.

To that end, I find that I don't just read books on business; I eat them, devouring every word. When I finish one that I truly enjoy, one which I have learned something from or in which I discovered words of wit and wisdom within its covers, I want to share it with like-minded individuals.

It is for this reason alone that I formulated this list to share with you. Take from it what you will; it is not me preaching or implying that you need to read them all. This list is just that—a list of books I have read over the years that have spoken to me. My wish is that some of them may do the same for you. Enjoy!

DON'S SUGGESTED READING LIST

- *I Love Capitalism!* Ken Langone, 2018, Penguin Random House

- *The Power of Positive Thinking*, Norman Vincent Peale, 1952, Prentice Hall

- *Good to Great*, Jim Collins, 2001, HarperCollins Publishers

- *Zero to One*, Peter Thiel, 2014, Crown Publishing Group

- *Building a StoryBrand*, Donald Miller, 2017, HarperCollins Publishers

- *Outliers*, Malcolm Gladwell, 2008, Little, Brown and Company

- *The 10X Rule*, Grant Cardone, 2011, John Wiley & Sons, Inc.

- *David and Goliath*, Malcolm Gladwell, 2013, Little, Brown and Company

- *Fanatical Prospecting*, Jeb Blount, 2015, John Wiley & Sons, Inc.

- *Start with No*, Jim Camp, 2002, Crown Publishing Group

- *Traction*, Gino Wickman, 2007, BenBella Books

- *Why the Best Are the Best*, Kevin Eastman, 2018, Advantage Media Group

- *How the Mighty Fall*, Jim Collins, 2009, HarperCollins Publishers

- *The No Asshole Rule*, Robert Sutton, 2007, Grand Central Publishing

- *Principles*, Ray Dalio, 2017, Simon & Schuster

- *The Voltage Effect*, John A. List, 2022, Penguin Random House

- *McDonald's: Behind the Arches*, John F. Love, 1986, Bantam Books

- *The Five Dysfunctions of a Team*, Patrick Lencioni, 2002, Jossey-Bass

- The Holy Bible, Scofield Reference, 1967, Oxford University Press

- *Playing to Win*, Alan G. Lafley and Roger L. Martin, 2013, Harvard Business Press

- *Blue Ocean Strategy*, W. Chan Kim and Renée Mauborgne, 2015, Harvard Business School Publishing Corporation

- *The Sales Development Playbook*, Trish Bertuzzi, 2013, Moore-Lake

If you like this list, or if you would like to suggest some of your own titles, I would love to hear from you. Please email me at *AlwaysTrust YourCape@vanquishfencing.com*. I truly enjoy learning how others are making their way in the entrepreneurial world of business.

A LITTLE EXTRA

Looking back on the last forty-some years of my life and business career—twenty or so prior to VANQUISH and twenty plus years in business for myself—I realized, to say the least, there were a few lessons learned. Some common sense, perhaps. Some shared with me directly by other people. Others were gained by way of reading books authored by great business observers and educators. Still others were forged by my own experiences, the school of hard knocks. In the pages of this book, you will have observed that I formulated these experiences into rules or lessons learned. In some cases, I referred to them as nonnegotiables, which I now describe more accurately as "channel markers." These channel markers have helped me as I navigated the river of life. I have listed them for you at the end of each chapter in which I feel they apply to the lessons described in that respective chapter. And for easy reference, I record them here in the following final pages of this book. And in so doing I offer you this thought as the builder of my business: the journey has now culminated in what I believe is a successful career as an entrepreneur.

In presenting my channel markers, I claim no pride of ownership. I offer them to you to do with as you see fit. I tried to explain how they were developed by me and what and who inspired me to add them to this list when it happened.

Most rules are written in blood. Meaning they are a result of something happening not as expected, and therefore, making a rule was necessary in hopes of preventing the less desirable outcome from happening again.

I suggest that you do not take these channel markers as gospel; your results and modifications of them should lead to your own unique outcomes. Rather, use them as marking points to spur your own thinking about your business and your life and use them to stimulate your own ideas for consideration when faced with decisions about your business and its growth path. Please make your own channel markers; although I feel as business owners and entrepreneurs, we face very similar challenges, your experiences will be individual to you and your business model and style.

When reviewing this list, remember the words of John Wooden, who is considered one of the greatest college basketball coaches: "Everything we know, we learned from someone else!"

Don's Channel Markers for Life and Business, Outlined from the Book

1. First things first.

I have observed so many people spending so much time working inefficiently. My conclusions told me that if I would just take the time to plan, I would accomplish so much more with the relatively short amount of time I have available. When I was in the army, there was a saying: "There is never enough time to do it right, but there is always enough time to do it again."

2. Don't build a box of responsibility until you are ready to live in it.

I learned this rule the hard way. It is so easy to say yes and so much harder to say no. Bottom line: the more responsibility I accept today directly limits my freedom in the future. Some call this the *opportunity cost*. Or worse, the results of the expectation of immediate gratification.

3. **Go after what I want in life; if I don't, I will never have it.**

When I left the army in 1981, I was faced with the question I had heard before and would hear again: "What will you do?" I had to develop the mindset that if I don't pursue what I want, I am sure not to have it. I have got to give it all that I have, and in some cases, more than I have will not be enough. But if I don't try, I will surely never have it.

4. **I will forever remain in the same spot If I don't step forward.**

I met so many people in my life who were afraid to take a chance, to get out of their comfort zone. The only way I was going to get out of the job I did not like or the relationship that was not working was if I made the change and that change came in the action of moving forward.

5. **Strive to control my future, or someone else will.**

My father and the army drove this lesson into my brain. In my early life as a son, as an enlisted man, as an employee, I was living someone else's dream and I was controlled by them as long as I was beholden to them for my survival.

6. **I must control my own destiny, or someone else will.**

I decided it was important for me to find a way to control my own destiny. I did it as best as I could while working for others, but I never truly experienced it until I started my own business.

This rule was also inspired by Jack Welch and his mother, who taught it to him. (Not to be confused with the channel marker above: controlling my destiny is much bigger than controlling my future!)

7. I can do anything, but I cannot do everything. I need to choose wisely.

I love the feeling of being able to do anything I want. The reality is that once I start down that path, my options almost always become limited. Therefore, I need to be sure, before I start, that I really want what I am about to do.

8. Use the power of thinking positively each day. Plan for the worst but expect the best.

When I discovered the book by Norman Vincent Peale, I was floored by his words. I practiced his ideas as a youth with great results and so it has made me an optimist by nature for life. The negative can and will happen, but I have learned to plan for the worst and expect the best.

9. Don't tell my audience everything just because I was asked to.

Telling my story to the Rotary Club helped me realize that I didn't fit into a box. I had done things that the Princeton boys and girls had never done, and I was okay with that. But in the future, I wouldn't tell my audience everything just because I was asked to.

10. Knowing my fatal flaw—I have to recognize, admit, and have a solid understanding of what can put me out of business—immediately.

I need to know my kryptonite! I need to determine what could defeat my business plan, and just as important, I need to identify a strategy to overcome this when it happens.

11. Don't solve a problem with a problem.

So many products on the market, especially in my market space, solve one problem only to create two more as a result of the first solution. This is a major no-no when building a start-up company new to the market.

12. Take educated and calculated risks, not thoughtless risks.

Based on the simple principle of "I should look before I leap" that was taught to me by my mom at a very young age, coupled with the risk/reward calculations of every safety officer I had ever employed—and in keeping with my own survival instincts—I need to think before I don my cape and jump.

13. I had to have my spouse's strong, unwavering support to start my business.

My spouse needs to be wholeheartedly in tune with and okay with the idea that I am going to start a business. The money will be tight, the hours will be long, and there are a whole host of things that can and will go wrong. It is extremely important that my spouse has a clear understanding of what I am about to do and be willing to deal with the pain that will come with starting my own business.

14. A clear and honest understanding of my personal abilities, talents, and especially limitations.

I have to be real with myself. I need to know what I am good at and what I am lacking in. I need to stand in front of the mirror and take a full self-evaluation of my skills, my knowledge, and, most importantly, my limitations. I need to have a strong belief in myself to know when times get tough, I will know how to seek help.

15. A business idea that appeals to my market space, solves a problem, and stands up to competition.

This is important! Just because it sounds like a good idea does not make it a good idea. My business has to, from day one, appeal to the market I want to sell to, it has to solve a problem, and it has got to be able to hold its own when compared to a competitor or a competitive product already in the market space. If it doesn't do all three of these things at a minimum, there is a good chance no one will buy what I am selling, and my business will fail.

16. The best problems to work on are often the ones nobody else even tries to solve.

When searching for a business to create and a market to secure for my company's future, it became very clear very early in the process that I needed to be in a niche market. I needed to address a problem most others did not try to solve. This advantage allowed me to operate effectively below the radar for twenty years. Long enough for me to establish my company as the original thought leader in the industry.

17. Build your brand from the start.

This is important. Once I determined what my product and service was, I needed to decide on two things: (1) how I was going to brand it so that everyone knew what it is that my company did, and (2) what my brand was and how I was going to promote it and protect it. McDonald's brand was "good food fast," and its branding was "You deserve a break today." Two very different items; both are in the category of branding from the start. In my case, how I presented my brand—"VANQUISH, protecting utility assets at the substation level with perimeter fencing systems that prevent small crawling animals from gaining access to a protected area"—and my branding in the marketplace—"VANQUISH: ALWAYS ON GUARD."

18. My business must have one clear underlying idea for a product, or a service and I must make it or do it the best I possibly can from day one.

I saw so many businesses start out trying to be everything to everyone in hope of finding something that works. The saying "less is more" is the strategic approach I decided on. My plan was to do one thing great, then do another thing great. I did not try to be a lot of things from the start because I felt it would dilute my offering if I only did them halfway. I believed if I focused on one thing, it would be done right and, to my preference, done great from the start!

19. Don't reinvent the mousetrap; build a better mousetrap.

This statement floated in the syllabus of most all the college classes I took in night school. So when I started my company, I researched what the so-called alternative solutions were in the market space I was going to sell into and designed my products and services to improve upon what others did wrong.

20. Improve on the competition.

Simple, but valuable to follow. I found that I wanted to be in a space where money is being spent on a problem but that there was no clear winner in solving the problem. That way, if I was able to supply a product or a service that works, I knew companies already budgeted and spend money; all I needed to do was capture it by improving on what the competition was not doing right.

21. Don't settle for good; strive for great in all that I do.

This rule is inspired by Jim Collins, after I read his argument that *good* is the enemy of *great*—simply because it is too easy to settle for *good*.

22. Keep the company lean and flexible.

I knew that because of a lack of capital, I was going to have a lean company from the start. I also knew that when it was just me on the payroll, I could be flexible. As I grew the business and the cash flow, the money became a little easier to come by. I always ran the fear of adding too many people and becoming too ingrained in how we do things to stay flexible.

23. Work in the three dimensions of success: learn from the past, produce in the present, prepare for the future.

In the process of building a business, especially one from nothing, I found that I needed to maintain a focus on what was really important. I needed to learn from the past experiences; I needed to manufacture or produce in the present while continually preparing for the future of my company. This rule is universal for any stage of the build I am in.

24. Reward yourself when you accomplish major milestones.

I had a boss once who taught me that when I had a great success in business, I should reward myself. Go to dinner, have a drink, buy a car, build a house, enjoy a bottle of wine—do something to reward yourself. For two reasons: (1) you remember the win when things don't go your way, and (2) you will entice yourself to desire the win again by accomplishing another of your major milestones.

25. Face reality as it is, not as it was or as we wish it were.

This rule was also inspired by Jack Welch and my dad. Both men harped on living in the reality of things. My dad would say, "Don't feel sorry for yourself, son; get up, face reality, deal with it." I have now and forever adapted that attitude in life and in business. I cannot make choices for my business based on what I would like to see in the real world. I need to make choices on what I know to be real in the world today.

26. I am not a failure if I do not reach my intended goal.

Although I strive every day to succeed, I must remember that if I fail today, it does not make me a failure. VANQUISH and I are only declared failures when we give up and stop trying.

27. Invest in my research.

Pretty self-explanatory, yet I found I needed to remind myself to invest back a portion of my earnings, especially in the early years when money was the tightest. I found I needed to continually learn new ways and to develop improvements based on the results of my research.

28. Invest in myself.

Here again, since I was, in the beginning, the only employee, I needed to be investing in educating myself. Which, truth be told, even after twenty years I still need to invest in myself. I need continual education on processes, products, and people, what I called the three *P*s of my business.

29. Invest in my business.

It would be nice if I made one investment, started the business, and then just sat back and reaped the rewards of that investment. Unfortunately, it doesn't work like that. I needed to make a commitment to reinvest in both time and money if I wanted my business to grow past the point of just making a living for myself. I looked at my business as a living, breathing life form, and it needed to be fed so it could grow into a more productive member of my life and my marketplace. I wanted, I needed, VANQUISH to be a self-sustaining entity someday, and that required an investment to be made every day.

30. Learn the language of corrective criticism, and develop a hunger for the process.

My mechanical drawing teacher in high school taught me the value of corrective criticism when he marked my drawings with his red pen for the first time. He made me realize that the only way to learn, to improve my production, is to see where I am deficient. Most times, that comes from someone criticizing my actions, my plan, my ideas. The trick is to not take it personally. To listen to the opposing thoughts being presented, evaluate them, incorporate them, or discard them as I see fit. I learned to listen to the language of corrective criticism.

31. Learn to listen.

This is one I struggle with to this day. I know I should listen more, but I find myself always talking, and when I am doing that, I am not learning. Listening keeps me humble. It also helps me to learn. It improves my relationships with my employees and my customers. By truly listening, I understand what they need from me, and that affords me the opportunity to grow the business.

32. Be teachable.

Being teachable goes hand in hand with corrective criticism. Mr. Raymond Cox instilled these words in me. He convinced me that I had to "always want to learn." Learn how to run a paper route, work at a hardware store, stack lumber on a truck, repair bicycles, as a kid. Years later, learn how to drive a truck, trade stocks on Wall Street, develop a financial plan. Being teachable is instinct for some, but for me, I believe I had to develop it within myself.

33. Embrace the learning process.

Education is key to success. Recognizing what I don't know is the first step in the learning process. It is equally important for me to understand what I am missing in my thought process as it is for me to effectively search it out and educate myself. In today's environment, education abounds, and all we have to do is seek to learn by embracing the learning process.

34. If you share with a competitor, you lose. Share with no one perceived to be a competitor.

This rule was learned the hard way. It is safer to assume that every perceived competitor or alternative solutions provider is out to steal my intellectual property. Therefore I should strive to protect it at all costs.

35. Intellectual property rights, patents, are only as good as my pockets are deep enough to defend them in court.

The old adage from my youth, "My father is bigger than your father," is the best way I know to explain this: the bigger the law firm they have, the harder it is to stop them from stealing from me. The money I spend to get patents and to defend patents needs to be considered before investing in future patents for my ideas.

36. My strategy for competing in the market space I choose must involve a different set of activities designed to deliver superior value to my customers, if I am to grow my business.

I must make the way I think about the value proposition I put into the universe different from my competitors if I am to offer a superior value for my customer's investment dollars. This rule was inspired by Mike Porter, author of *Competitive Strategy*, and introduced to me by the authors of *Playing to Win*.

37. Dream so big that I make those around me uncomfortable.

This rule is based on the popular BHAG principle: do the impossible by setting Big Hairy Audacious Goals for yourself and your team. The example often cited is the goal of being the first to land on the moon in the early 1960s.

38. My business needs to adapt to changing markets, or it will cease to exist.

This rule was also inspired by Jack Welch. His rule read: "If the rate of change on the outside exceeds the rate of change on the inside, the end is near."

39. The answer will always be no if I don't ask for what I want.

Pretty simple rule, but I am amazed at how many times in my life I did not ask, and therefore I did not receive. In life, in business, and specifically in sales, if I don't ask for the order, I will surely never get it. So I developed a habit of asking for the order every time. I did not always get it, but I believe I am a success today because I got a yes more times than I got a no, which was certain if I did not ask.

40. If I don't have a competitive advantage, I don't compete.

This rule was also inspired by Jack Welch. If I cannot be number one or number two in my space, I should not compete. When the three multinational fence manufacturers invaded my market space for a specific security solution, I moved my company's focus away from the shining object of their desire. This process allowed me to keep the lion's share of the customers' business in my space while conceding the smaller market to the competition, which ultimately eliminated their ability to compete with me.

41. Whatever I do in business and in life, I need to lean into it.

The outcome, good or bad, doesn't matter as much as the fact that I have put my all into it, whatever it is. The only chance I have to succeed is by showing up and being completely committed, there in that moment.

42. I need a really good knock if I am ever going to get people to listen to me.

Most doors in the world are closed to me, so when I find one that I want to go through, I better be damn sure I have an interesting knock.

43. If I like something because I think other people are going to like it, it's a sure bet no one will.

Pretty self-explanatory, but just the same, I need to be original in my thinking and do something because it adds value to me and to those I am willing to share my thoughts and actions with.

44. Everything I think is important isn't. Everything I think is unimportant turns out to be important.

Again, pretty self-explanatory. Unfortunately, my experiences have recorded this as happening to me more often than I care to admit. Underscoring my need to think hard and long about the actions I am about to take.

45. The quality of what I sell should be second to none and should be my primary goal.

I never want to sell an inferior product just to gain market share. I always sell a quality product at a quality price. I focus my efforts to maintain the best possible product and service I can give.

46. Make what you offer worth the purchase price to the customer, and sales will come.

I want my product and service to always be considered second to none. This strategy allows me to deliver a quality return on investment for my client, which, to my way of thinking, will drive sales. I never want to be so focused on making the sale that I diminish the VANQUISH brand.

47. "Every Day We Make It, We Will Make It the Best We Can."

I adopted this rule after visiting the Jack Daniel's Distillery in Lynchburg, Tennessee, and saw Jack's version hanging in what was once his office. I think the rule needs no explanation.

48. Seek out and make teachable moments count.

As I move from being the boss, the manager of people, to being the leader of my people, my team, I need to invest in them as individuals. A large part of the investment is finding teachable moments and using those moments to educate and lead the behavior I want in my organization. My people and I need to learn to recognize those moments and to be teachable in order to grow.

49. I cannot let the fear of change cause me to miss an opportunity.

I have to be constantly monitoring the business climate in which VANQUISH operates so that I do not miss the market changes. I need to adapt to those changes in order to stay relevant to my customers, not only today but, more importantly, tomorrow as well. Otherwise, I may find my business going out of business. This rule was loosely inspired by Jack Welch when he said "Change before we have to."

50. Invest in my people.

Think in the "we," not in the "I," mindset. I believed from the start that "I" was a "we" and that "we" would be a team at VANQUISH one day, and that once I started to invite people to play in my sandbox, I needed to have a way to invest in them so that they would be the most productive members of the team. At first this investment was their paychecks. But in short order, it became an investment in education and, to a larger degree, an investment of my time to coach and lead them to productivity.

51. Make the investment to win.

I believed that I needed to make specific choices to win in the marketplace. A. G. Lafley, former chairman and CEO of Procter & Gamble, along with Roger L. Martin, dean of the Rotman School of Management, said it best in their book, *Playing to Win*, "A company must seek to win in a particular place and in a particular way. If it doesn't seek to win, it is wasting the time of its people and the investments of its capital provider." In the case of VANQUISH, it is my capital. By making this one of my rules, I chose to make the investment to win.

52. Make incremental advances.

As my product line advanced, I would continually study its effectiveness, and as necessary, I made continuous improvements to the actual product and the way I presented it. Basically, I tweaked every aspect of my service, my products, and my business to be sure they were all the very best they could be based on the knowledge I had at that moment in time. Once I had better data, I improved based on that new knowledge continually.

53. Look where I want to go, not where I am going.

Regardless of where business is today, I find that, just like riding my motorcycle, I need to look where I want my business to go, in the direction of my goals. So that my team and I will make decisions today that will ultimately lead the business toward the achievement of those goals in the future.

54. It is more important for me to be a great leader than it is to be a great boss.

I need to be the visionary, the keeper of the dream, and to lead my team to take us in the direction of change and growth if VANQUISH is to survive and thrive. This rule was loosely inspired by Jack Welch. His rule read: Be powerful in the knowledge that I have asked the right questions.

55. Leave my ego at the door.

I have observed that some entrepreneurs get to a point where they believe they know more than anyone else and that they are somehow smarter than the rest. To my way of thinking, this is a very dangerous position to be in. Therefore, this rule is for me to leave my ego at the door and learn to listen as well as I hear.

56. The right people are my most important asset.

This rule is based on the principles I learned from Collins in *Good to Great*, in which he talks about Level 5 leaders and the importance of having the right people on the bus and in the right seats before you decide where to drive the bus.

57. Practice intellectual honesty.

This rule came to me via Peter Drucker, a management consultant, educator, and author whose writings contributed to the philosophical and practical foundations of modern business. Combined with Jack Welch's "Reality Principle," they form the basis of teams working together for the greater good of the business. Our management team members must be honest with each other and trust each other if they are to lead the organization to great success.

58. Be candid with everyone.

This rule flows out of the "Practice intellectual honesty" rule. Management team members must be candid and honest with each other if they are to create harmony within the organization. This rule was inspired by Jack Welch.

59. Don't manage; lead.

In order for my business to grow, I need to be the visionary, the leader, the one who speaks inspiration into the mission of the company. Therefore I need to lead my team to determine the means to success. I cannot manage them to success.

60. Face reality as it is, not as it was or as I wish it were.

This rule was also inspired by Jack Welch and my dad. Both men harped on living in the reality of things. My dad would say, "Don't feel sorry for yourself, son; get up, face reality, deal with it." I have, now and forever, adapted that attitude in life and in business. I cannot make choices for my business based on what I would like to see in the real world. I need to make choices on what I know to be real in the world today.

61. I need to build my entrepreneurial muscle memory every day so that when I need it, I will not have to stop to think. I will instinctively act.

Watch athletes, especially good ones. They practice for hours, repeating the same action over and over again, building what they call *muscle memory*. When in a game and the moment comes to take the shot or make the throw, they don't think; they just act. I believe that as a leader of my business, I need to practice every day so that when the time comes, I know how to respond. I need to build my muscle memory, just like the athletes.

62. Resistance is needed to grow.

I have found that, just like weightlifters in the gym, I need to feel resistance when working out to grow my muscles. My business and my leadership team needs to feel the wind in our faces, pushing back, in order to keep us sharp, growing, and focused and to know we are going in the right direction. When the wind is always at our back, we have a tendency to get weak and to lose focus on the goal.

63. Bonus rule: I must believe in myself and my abilities.

Or put another way: Always Trust Your Cape!

ABOUT VANQUISH

For over twenty years, VANQUISH, the original animal mitigation specialist, has offered exceptional quality and supreme value. We pride ourselves on being an innovator in the field and look forward to continuing to work with electric utilities to solve problems in the future.

Our vision is to provide barriers that create a safe and secure environment, intimidating to intruders while adding to the overall appearance and protection of assets. Every day we make it, we will make it the best we can.

INGENUITY

Design safe, long-lasting solutions.

INTEGRITY

Real in all we do, by offering superior solutions at reasonable margins.

PASSION

Unrivaled vision, innovation, and execution.

QUALITY

We're here to help, from concept to installation.

The VANQUISH Difference

Others claim their product good, but ours does what you think it should. VANQUISH Non-Conductive Fencing Systems: widely regarded as an improved beautification solution.